Getting Started with Mule Cloud Connect
Accelerating Integration with SaaS, Social Media, and Open APIs

Ryan Carter

Beijing · Cambridge · Farnham · Köln · Sebastopol · Tokyo

Getting Started with Mule Cloud Connect

by Ryan Carter

Printed in the United States of America.

Published by O'Reilly Media, Inc., 1005 Gravenstein Highway North, Sebastopol, CA 95472.

O'Reilly books may be purchased for educational, business, or sales promotional use. Online editions are also available for most titles (*http://my.safaribooksonline.com*). For more information, contact our corporate/institutional sales department: 800-998-9938 or *corporate@oreilly.com*.

Editors: Andy Oram and Mike Hendrickson	**Cover Designer:** Karen Montgomery
Production Editor: Kara Ebrahim	**Interior Designer:** David Futato
Proofreader: Kara Ebrahim	**Illustrator:** Kara Ebrahim

December 2012:   First Edition

Revision History for the First Edition:

2012-12-19:   First release

2013-01-04:   Second release

2014-05-23:   Third release

See *http://oreilly.com/catalog/errata.csp?isbn=9781449331009* for release details.

ISBN: 978-1-449-33100-9

[LSI]

Table of Contents

Preface

There's no question that we are undergoing a generational shift in computing. With the massive adoption of social media, SaaS, and cloud computing, enterprises are relying more and more on resources beyond the firewall. With this shift, we have seen an explosion in the number of open APIs that are required to interact with these new services. These APIs are key to unlocking the wealth of data and functionality out there. But with this comes serious challenges, with the leading one being integration.

Enterprise application integration (EAI) is a term coined by Gartner, Inc. in 1998 and defined as "the unrestricted sharing of data and business processes among any connected application or data sources in the enterprise. " The challenge is no longer to connect the data sources "within" the enterprise, but instead to connect data sources from a myriad of places, both inside and outside the enterprise.

From Messaging to Connectivity

Typical "Enterprise" message bus and broker implementation's for integrating on-premise applications are no longer suitable for these Web 2.0 style APIs. I have worked with many of these implementations over the years, including Mule since early in version 2, implementing SOA and message broking solutions and working with technologies and protocols such as SOAP, CORBA, and JMS. However, with this recent shift, it's less about messaging and more about just staying connected, working natively with Web technologies and protocols such as REST, JSON, and OAuth. This is where Mule differs. As I have adapted to these new technologies, so has Mule. It has grown up with me. When I need to integrate a new technology or SaaS provider, Mule has gotten there before me and there's already a connector for it.

This book aims to introduce you to Mule, and more specifically, Mule Cloud Connect. With step-by-step instructions to get you to build your own connectors, this book will walk you through working with some of the most popular APIs from social media to

SaaS and show you how to easily get started with the latest Web API trends including REST, OAuth, and real-time technologies.

Conventions Used in This Book

The following typographical conventions are used in this book:

Italic

> Indicates new terms, URLs, email addresses, filenames, and file extensions.

`Constant width`

> Used for program listings, as well as within paragraphs to refer to program elements such as variable or function names, databases, data types, and environment variables.

`Constant width italic`

> Shows text that should be replaced with user-supplied values or by values determined by context.

 This icon indicates a warning or caution.

Using Code Examples

This book is here to help you get your job done. In general, if this book includes code examples, you may use the code in your programs and documentation. You do not need to contact us for permission unless you're reproducing a significant portion of the code. For example, writing a program that uses several chunks of code from this book does not require permission. Selling or distributing a CD-ROM of examples from O'Reilly books does require permission. Answering a question by citing this book and quoting example code does not require permission. Incorporating a significant amount of example code from this book into your product's documentation does require permission.

We appreciate, but do not require, attribution. An attribution usually includes the title, author, publisher, and ISBN. For example: "*Getting Started with Mule Cloud Connect* by Ryan Carter (O'Reilly). Copyright 2013 Ryan Carter, 978-1-449-33100-9."

If you feel your use of code examples falls outside fair use or the permission given above, feel free to contact us at *permissions@oreilly.com*.

Safari® Books Online

 Safari Books Online (*www.safaribooksonline.com*) is an on-demand digital library that delivers expert content in both book and video form from the world's leading authors in technology and business.

Technology professionals, software developers, web designers, and business and creative professionals use Safari Books Online as their primary resource for research, problem solving, learning, and certification training.

Safari Books Online offers a range of product mixes and pricing programs for organizations, government agencies, and individuals. Subscribers have access to thousands of books, training videos, and prepublication manuscripts in one fully searchable database from publishers like O'Reilly Media, Prentice Hall Professional, Addison-Wesley Professional, Microsoft Press, Sams, Que, Peachpit Press, Focal Press, Cisco Press, John Wiley & Sons, Syngress, Morgan Kaufmann, IBM Redbooks, Packt, Adobe Press, FT Press, Apress, Manning, New Riders, McGraw-Hill, Jones & Bartlett, Course Technology, and dozens more. For more information about Safari Books Online, please visit us online.

How to Contact Us

Please address comments and questions concerning this book to the publisher:

O'Reilly Media, Inc.
1005 Gravenstein Highway North
Sebastopol, CA 95472
800-998-9938 (in the United States or Canada)
707-829-0515 (international or local)
707-829-0104 (fax)

We have a web page for this book, where we list errata, examples, and any additional information. You can access this page at *http://oreil.ly/mule-cloud*.

To comment or ask technical questions about this book, send email to *bookquestions@oreilly.com*.

For more information about our books, courses, conferences, and news, see our website at *http://www.oreilly.com*.

Find us on Facebook: *http://facebook.com/oreilly*

Follow us on Twitter: *http://twitter.com/oreillymedia*

Watch us on YouTube: *http://www.youtube.com/oreillymedia*

Content Updates

January 4, 2013

- Chapter 1: Updated code samples to remove the extra ":" typo in `http:inbound-endpoint`s and to unescape ampersands.
- Chapter 4: Updated all code samples to include new namespace declarations for the latest Mule object store module. Updated LinkedIn code samples to work with the latest release of the LinkedIn connector, changing the operation names for saving and restoring OAuth tokens. Updated Twitter code samples to work with the latest release of the Twitter connector (removing the response `format` attribute).
- Chapter 5: Updated all SalesForce code samples to include an `http:inbound-endpoint` for triggering flows.
- Chapter 6: Updated Twitter code samples to work with the latest release of the Twitter connector (removing the response `format` attribute).

May 23, 2014

- Chapter 1: General tidying up and updates to text and code samples.
- Chapter 2: General tidying up and updates to text and code samples.
- Chapter 3: Added a new chapter demonstrating orchestration and transformation.
- Chapter 4: Previously Chapter 3; moved to accomodate new chapter. Added new OAuth functionalty for Mule 3.4 and 3.5 and improvements.
- Chapter 5: Previously Chapter 4; moved to accomodate new chapter.
- Chapter 6: Previously Chapter 5; moved to accomodate new chapter. Added new sections for new features for Mule 3.4 and 3.5, including schedulers and watermarking. Updated code samples and general tidying up.
- Chapter 7: Previously Chapter 6; moved to accomodate new chapter.

Acknowledgments

Many people have helped this book happen. Many thanks go to Andy Oram, the editor of the book at O'Reilly Media, Ross Mason, who helped shape and organize the book, Emiliano Lesende for all the technical help, all other technical reviewers including David Dossot, Tom Stroobants, and Victor Romero, and all the other Muleys in the community.

CHAPTER 1

Getting Started

It all starts with a simple API that publishes someone's status to Facebook, sends a Tweet, or updates a contact in Salesforce. As you start to integrate more and more of these external services with your applications, trying to identify the tasks that one might want to perform when you're surrounded by SOAP, REST, JSON, XML, GETs, PUTs, POSTs, and DELETEs, can be a real challenge.

Open APIs are all about endpoints. Most services follow the current trend of providing a RESTful endpoint, others use older RPC-based protocols such as SOAP or XML-RPC, some use newer "real-time," push-focused endpoints like WebSockets or HTTP Streaming, others may offer a number of different endpoints to meet different requirements, and some just use what seems to be best for a specific job, which might mean not strictly following protocol rules. This is one of the biggest challenges with open APIs: inconsistency. Figure 1-1 shows the estimated popularity of different styles of APIs.

Each API is different, with different data formats and authorization mechanisms. One API's interpretation of REST may even differ from another. One reason for this is the nature of REST itself. The RESTful principles come from a paper published by Roy Fielding in 2000 and since then RESTful services have dominated SOAP-based services on the web year after year. Although REST services have many advantages over SOAP-based services, the original paper only included a set of constraints and provides no specification about how to define a RESTful API and handle things like URI schemes, authentication, error handling, and more.

By observing the vastly different opinions out there, there is no one right way to define a web API, which has resulted in many inconsistencies, even between APIs from the same service provider. Top that off with the remaining SOAP services and newer technologies such as HTTP Streaming and you're left with a lot of different API styles and protocols to learn. Working with all these APIs can just be too damn hard, and this is where Mule Cloud Connect comes in. Mule Cloud Connectors, recently renamed to

Anypoint Connectors are a powerful, lightweight toolset providing a consistent interface to a large number of cloud, SaaS, social media, and Web APIs.

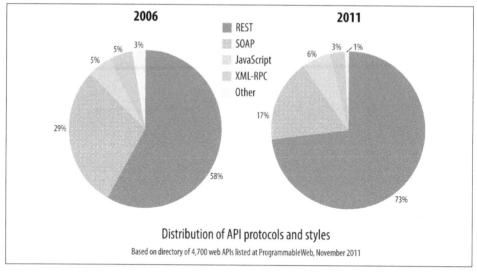

Figure 1-1. Distribution of API protocols

Cloud Connectors Versus the REST of the World

There are many different levels of working with APIs. To put Cloud Connectors into context, let's first look at some other approaches to integrating APIs.

To demonstrate, we will use the GeoNames API (*http://www.geonames.org/*). GeoNames is a worldwide geographical database that contains over 10 million geographical names. I tend to use GeoNames because it's easy to consume (providing both XML and JSON formats) and does not require any account setup for demo purposes.

Transport-Specific Clients

Transport-specific clients deal directly with APIs over the wire. These clients deal with the actual bytes that pass between your application and the external API. For a RESTful service, it requires you to build a URL and associate it with the correct URI parameters and HTTP headers. For a SOAP-based service, it requires you to build the contents of the HTTP POST yourself, including the SOAP:Envelope and any WS-* content. Example 1-1 shows a very simple Java snippet for constructing a simple client for a RESTful service using Java's HTTP packages.

Example 1-1. RESTful Java client with java.net URL

```
URL url = new URL("http://api.geonames.org/findNearbyJSON" +
                  "?lat=37.51&amp;lng=-122.18&amp;username=demo");

HttpURLConnection conn = (HttpURLConnection) url.openConnection();
conn.setRequestMethod("GET");
conn.setRequestProperty("Accept", "application/json");

if (conn.getResponseCode() != 200) {
    throw new RuntimeException("Failed : HTTP error code : " + conn.getResponse
Code());
}

BufferedReader  br  =  new  BufferedReader(new  InputStreamReader(conn.getInput
Stream()));

String output;
while ((output = br.readLine()) != null) {
    System.out.println(output);
}

conn.disconnect();
```

This is the most abstract way of working with APIs. The semantics of HTTP libraries match the HTTP protocol and not REST or SOAP APIs specifically. This leaves it up to you to construct URLs, build up request structures, and write them to and from input and output streams, requiring you to know the API very well.

When you start working with more complex APIs that require connection or state management, you're left to do this manually, which is error prone and requires far more effort to handle reliably.

Language-Specific Clients

Language-specific libraries, such as Jersey clients for Rest APIs or Apache CXF for SOAP APIs, wrap the underlying protocols in methods that are more familiar and comfortable for programmers in that language. For example, Example 1-2 shows a very simple code snippet for using Jersey to invoke RESTful service.

Example 1-2. Jersey REST client

```
WebResource webResource = client.resource("http://api.geonames.org/findNearbyJSON");
MultivaluedMap queryParams = new MultivaluedMapImpl();
queryParams.add("lat", "lat");
queryParams.add("lng", "-122.18");
queryParams.add("username", "demo");
String s = webResource.queryParams(queryParams).get(String.class);
```

Using this example, the Jersey client libraries abstract away a lot of the HTTP specifics and make API clients a lot clearer by providing short code that helps express the semantics of the particular API protocol. This is one advantage over using transports, but you're still left importing WSDLs for SOAP services and object binding to and from request structures. If you're using multiple protocols, you may have to learn and maintain multiple libraries. Because they are generic and not specific to any particular API, you will still have to write custom code to work with each API's little idiosyncrasies or custom features such as session-based authentication and OAuth.

Service-Specific Client Libraries

A client library specifically developed for a particular API, such as Twitter4j for the Twitter APIs, makes things easier by extracting away a lot of the protocol and transport specifics. Example 1-3 shows an example of working with GeoNames' Java library.

Example 1-3. Service-specific client library

```
WebService.setUserName("demo");
ToponymSearchCriteria searchCriteria = new ToponymSearchCriteria();
searchCriteria.setQ("zurich");
ToponymSearchResult searchResult = WebService.search(searchCriteria);
for (Toponym toponym : searchResult.getToponyms()) {
    System.out.println(toponym.getName()+" "+ toponym.getCountryName());
}
```

Convenient as these are, because they fit the semantics of the service closely, they are typically developed by the individual service providers or developer communities. Therefore, there is no consistency between implementations.

Cloud/Anypoint Connectors

Mule Cloud/Anypoint Connectors offer a more maintainable way to work with APIs. Built on top of the Mule and CloudHub integration platforms, Connectors are service-specific clients that abstract away the complexities of transports and protocols. Many complex but common processes such as authorization and session management work without you having to write a single line of code. Although service-specific, Cloud Connectors all share a common and consistent interface to configure typical API tasks such as OAuth, WebHooks, and connection management. They remove the pain from working with multiple, individual client libraries. Example 1-4 shows a really basic example of configuring a Cloud Connector to access the GeoNames API, which will be covered in more detail shortly.

Example 1-4. Cloud Connector configuration

```
<geonames:config username="demo" />

<geonames:find-nearby-pois-osm latitude="37.451"
            longitude="-127" />
```

Connectors are essentially plain old Java objects (POJOs) developed by Mule and the community using an SDK called the DevKit. The DevKit is the successor to the original Cloud Connect SDK, which was developed with just external APIs in mind but has since been opened up to create any manner of Mule extension such as transformers or pretty much anything. The DevKit uses annotations that mimic typical integration tasks to simplify development, and when processed, are converted into fully featured components for the Mule ESB and CloudHub integration platforms.

Mule Cloud Connectors support many of the most widely-used web APIs from SaaS to social media, with more being developed every day. Current connectors include Twitter, Facebook, LinkedIn, Salesforce, Amazon WebServices, Twilio, and many more. A full categorized list of available connectors and what they offer can be found here (*http:// www.mulesoft.org/extensions*).

Mule: A Primer

Before diving straight into configuring connectors, it's important to understand some basic concepts. After this short overview, you'll be ready to build your first application and start taking advantage of Mule Cloud/Anypoint connectors. To begin, we will first build a simple Mule application that we can use as the base of our examples and introduce some core concepts for those unfamiliar with Mule.

As mentioned previously, Mule is an integration platform that allows developers to connect applications together quickly and easily, enabling them to exchange data regardless of the different technologies that the applications use. It is also at the core of CloudHub, an Integration Platform as a Service (IPaaS). CloudHub allows you to integrate cross-cloud services, create new APIs on top of existing data sources, and integrate on-premise applications with cloud services.

Later in the book we will look at specific connectors, but to start let's take a look at a simple API proxy that can be used to mediate an external service and introduce some transformation and some routing between the two. This application will expose a simple HTTP interface that can be invoked through a browser or HTTP client, contact an external service, and transform the returned response to the browser.

Mule Configuration

XML is the format for the files that control Mule. Built on top of the Spring framework (*http://projects.spring.io/spring-framework/*); it uses schemas and namespaces to provide a domain specific language (DSL) authoring environment. Mule also provides a dedicated IDE via Mule Studio. Mule Studio is an Eclipse based, graphical IDE for authoring Mule flows that reduces Mule configuration to a set of visual objects. It provides round-tripping between a visual representation of your flows and your XML configuration. Whether you use the graphical representation or XML, you will no doubt need to dive into the XML configuration at some point, so this book will primarily focus on the XML configuration. Example 1-5 shows the finished application.

Example 1-5. Simple Mule API proxy application

```xml
<?xml version="1.0" encoding="UTF-8"?>
<mule xmlns="http://www.mulesoft.org/schema/mule/core"
    xmlns:xsi="http://www.w3.org/2001/XMLSchema-instance"
    xmlns:spring="http://www.springframework.org/schema/beans"
    xmlns:http="http://www.mulesoft.org/schema/mule/http"
    xsi:schemaLocation="
        http://www.mulesoft.org/schema/mule/core
        http://www.mulesoft.org/schema/mule/core/current/mule.xsd
        http://www.mulesoft.org/schema/mule/http
        http://www.mulesoft.org/schema/mule/http/current/mule-http.xsd
        http://www.springframework.org/schema/beans
        http://www.springframework.org/schema/beans/spring-beans-3.0.xsd">

    <flow name="main">
        <http:inbound-endpoint host="localhost" port="8080" path="geonamesproxy"
            exchange-pattern="request-response" />

        <http:outbound-endpoint
            address="http://api.geonames.org/findNearbyPOIsOSM?lat=37.451
            &amp;lng=-122.18&amp;username=demo" method="GET" />
    </flow>
</mule>
```

Inspecting this configuration, we can see that it is an XML document with a root element of mule. This element is the key element and must always be included. It is this element that contains references to specific Mule modules, via schema and namespace declarations, to provide the DSL authoring environment. The most important of these is the core namespace, xmlns="http://www.mulesoft.org/schema/mule/core", which allows you to use all the Mule core components such as flows, routers, transformers, and filters. The core namespace is then followed by subsequent namespace declarations that represent individual Mule modules, such as the HTTP module represented by xmlns:http="http://www.mulesoft.org/schema/mule/http" and the Spring module represented by xmlns:spring="http://www.springframework.org/schema/beans".

Flows

Within the `mule` root element is a critical child element: `flow`. Flows are underlying configurations for your Mule or CloudHub integration and are the default constructs for orchestrating message processing. Each flow has a `name` attribute, which must be a unique identifier within your configuration. The flow then consists of a *message source* followed by a sequence of *message processors*. Flows are executed from top to bottom, just like any imperative programming language. Example 1-6 shows the flow we have created with the unique ID: `main`.

Example 1-6. A Mule flow

```
<flow name="main">
    <http:inbound-endpoint host="localhost" port="8080"
        path="geonamesproxy" exchange-pattern="request-response" />

    <http:outbound-endpoint
        address="http://api.geonames.org/findNearbyPOIsOSM?lat=37.451
        &amp;lng=-122.18&amp;username=demo" method="GET" />
</flow>
```

Message Sources

A message source appears at the beginning of a flow. It receives or generates messages and forwards them on to a set of message processors to start working with the message. The message source is typically an inbound endpoint, such as HTTP or JMS, which can listen or poll on a certain address. The flow in the previous example has an HTTP message source for listening on a specific HTTP port, as shown in Example 1-7.

Example 1-7. HTTP message source

```
<http:inbound-endpoint host="localhost" port="8080"
    path="geonamesproxy" exchange-pattern="request-response" />
```

In this case, we have added a `host` attribute with the value `localhost`, a `port` attribute with the value `8080`, and a `path` attribute with the value `geonamesproxy`. This flow, when run, will create a web server that will listen on *http://localhost:8080/geonamesproxy*.

Message Processors

With the message source in place, we now need some message processors to actually do something with the received message. A message processor is used by Mule to process any messages received by a message source. Each processor can be a transformer, a Java component, or an outbound endpoint to forward on the message to an external system or to another flow.

In this case, we want to forward the message on to the GeoNames API. The GeoNames API is a simple HTTP web API, so we can create an HTTP outbound endpoint similar to that of our message source to forward on the message:

```
<http:outbound-endpoint
        address="http://api.geonames.org/findNearbyPOIsOSM?lat=37.451
        &amp;lng=-122.18&amp;username=demo" method="GET" />
```

As you can see, this is very similar to the message source, with the most noticeable difference being that we have changed the element name from -inbound-endpoint to -outbound-endpoint. In this element we have then specified an address attribute with the value of one of the GeoNames APIs and some hard-coded query parameters:

```
http://api.geonames.org/findNearbyPOIsOSM?
lat=37.451&amp;lng=-122.18&amp;username=demo
```

The GeoNames API also requires the GET HTTP method, so we have included the method attribute on the endpoint and set its value to GET.

Variables and Expressions

To support the work of message processors, Mule provides the *Mule Expression Language* (MEL) to access, manipulate, and consume information from the message and its environment. Mule makes this data available via the following four contexts:

Server
> The operating system on which the message processor is running

Mule
> The Mule instance on which the application is running

Application
> The user application within which the current flow is deployed

Message
> The package (payload, attachments, properties) that the message processor is processing

These contexts are at the heart of most MEL expressions. A typical MEL expression combines one of these contexts with one or more operands and zero or more operators in a Java-like syntax and returns the resulting value. For example, to access the payload of the message, we can use the expression #[message.payload], where message represents the message context and payload represents the payload property within the specified context. The syntax consists of a preceding #[followed by the expression to execute and a terminating] character.

In most cases, MEL expressions work within message processors to modify the way those processors do their main jobs, such as routing and filtering based on the message content. The following sections will focus on using the message context and cover some of the main use-cases that will be used throughout the book.

Message properties

Aside from the payload of the message, which is typically the main body of a message, message processors such as inbound and outbound endpoints add additional headers to a message called *message properties*. Message properties are defined within the following two scopes:

Inbound properties
> Inbound properties are placed on a message receiving a request on an inbound endpoint or a response from an outbound endpoint. For example, if a message to an inbound endpoint is called via HTTP with a Content-Type header, this property will be placed as a property within the inbound scope.

Outbound properties
> Outbound properties are set on a message to be sent via an outbound endpoint. For example, if a message with an outbound property Content-Type is sent via HTTP, the Content-Type property will be placed as an HTTP header on the outbound message.

MEL expressions allow you to refer to these message properties via a java.util.Map interface. For each property scope, Mule associates a map containing each property with the current message. You can refer to these maps using the following syntax:

```
#[message.inboundProperties['someProperty']]
#[message.outboundProperties['someProperty']]
```

where inboundProperties and outboundProperties are the maps within the message context and *someProperty* is they key of the property you want to retrieve from the map. Example 1-8 amends our GeoNames example to extract the latitude query parameter from the incoming request to use as an input to the original GeoNames request URL.

Example 1-8. Using message properties

```
<flow name="main">
    <http:inbound-endpoint host="localhost" port="8080"
    path="geonamesproxy" exchange-pattern="request-response" />

    <http:outbound-endpoint
        address="http://api.geonames.org/findNearbyPOIsOSM
        ?lat=#[message.inboundProperties['latitude']]
        &amp;lng=-122.18&amp;username=demo" method="GET" />
</flow>
```

With the amended configuration in place, if you execute the flow with your browser using the URL *http://localhost:8080/geonamesproxy?latitude=37.451*, Mule will now propagate the `latitude` parameter to the `lat` argument in the GeoNames request URL.

Additional variables

Typically, message properties should be reserved for the Mule message for things such as HTTP headers or JMS headers. To store additional information during the execution of a flow, like variables in Java, Mule provides two more types of scoped variables:

Flow variables
> Flow variables are global to the current flow. They retain their values as control passes from one message processor to another. Thus, you can set them in one message processor and use them in another.

Session variables
> Session variables are essentially the same as flow variables, but in addition, when one flow calls another one via a Mule endpoint, they are propagated and are available in the subsequent flow.

As with message properties, flow and session variables are available via a `java.util.Map` interface. This map data can be referenced using the following syntax:

```
#[flowVars['someProperty']]
#[sessionVars['someProperty']]
```

Storing variable data

In order to store variable data, Mule provides a set of message processors to simplify working with each property or variable scope.

Setting properties. To set a message property, Mule provides the `set-property` message processor. This message property works only with outbound scoped properties as the inbound scoped properties are immutable. The following example shows how to set the `Content-Type` property on a message using this message processor:

```
<set-property propertyName="Content-Type" value="text/plain"/>
```

This message processor takes two mandatory arguments: `propertyName` and `value`. `propertyName` is the name of the property to set and `value` is the value of the property. Either of these arguments' values can also be expressions themselves. For example, to copy the `Content-Type` property from the inbound scope to the outbound scope, you could use the following example:

```
<set-property propertyName="Content-Type"
        value="#[message.inboundProperties['Content-Type']]"/>
```

Setting variables. As with properties, similar message processors are available for both flow and session variables. `set-variable` sets a flow variable and `set-session-variable` sets a session variable. The syntax for these message processors are very similar as the previous `set-property` message processor, with `variableName` being the name of the variable to set and `value` being the value of the variable. The following example demonstrates setting both flow and session variables:

```
<set-variable variableName="myFlowVariable" value="some data"/>

<set-session-variable variableName="mySessionVariable" value="some data"/>
```

Enrichment. Another way of setting message properties or variables is via enrichment. Mule provides an `enricher` element to enrich the current message with extra information. It allows you to call out to another resource and set extra information on the message without overriding the current payload of the message. For example, you can call out to another endpoint or message processor and store its return value in a message property or variable. The following example demonstrates this effect, using the enricher to call the GeoNames service and store the response in a message property:

```
<flow name="main">
    <http:inbound-endpoint host="localhost" port="8080"
        path="geonamesproxy" exchange-pattern="request-response" />


    <enricher target="#[message.outboundProperties['response']]">
        <http:outbound-endpoint
            address="http://api.geonames.org/findNearbyPOIsOSM
            ?lat=#[message.inboundProperties['latitude']]
            &amp;lng=-122.18&amp;username=demo" method="GET" />
    </enricher>
</flow>
```

The `target` attribute defines how the current message is enriched by using expressions to define where the value is stored on the message. Here we are using standard MEL syntax to refer to an outbound property using `#[message.outboundProperties['res ponse']`. This will add or overwrite the specified message property with the result of the outbound endpoint. The main difference between using the enricher and the `set-property` message processor is that the enricher supports setting the value of the property via a nested message processor such as an outbound endpoint, whereas the `set-property` and other associated message processors only support setting the value's `value` attribute. This just demonstrates the broad strokes of the procedure. More information on enrichment can be found here (*http://bit.ly/1nfApBw*).

Functions

In addition to getting or setting information within a specific context, Mule also provides an expression syntax for executing certain functions. Functions provide a way of extracting information that doesn't already exist as a single value within a particular context. For example, if you have an XML document and care only about a particular node or value within that document, you can use the xpath function to extract that particular value. Or if you want extract a specific part of a string, you can use the regex function, and so on.

 Xpath (*http://www.w3.org/TR/xpath/*) is a closely related sister specification of the XML document specification and provides a declarative query language for addressing parts of an XML document.

Our current configuration will return an XML-formatted document representing the GeoNames response. Example 1-9 demonstrates using a simple xpath expression to log the name of the root element.

Example 1-9. Using functions

```
<flow name="main">
    <http:inbound-endpoint host="localhost" port="8080"
        path="geonamesproxy" exchange-pattern="request-response" />

    <http:outbound-endpoint
        address="http://api.geonames.org/findNearbyPOIsOSM
        ?lat=#[message.inboundProperties['latitude']]
        &amp;lng=-122.18&amp;username=demo" method="GET" />

    <logger level="INFO" message="#[xpath('local-name(/*)')]" />
</flow>
```

Routing

Mule has always had support for many routing options. Routers in Mule implement the Enterprise Integration Patterns (EIP). They are message processors that determine how messages are directed within a flow.

Alongside MEL, routers can decide on a course of action based on the contents, properties, or context of a message. Example 1-10 demonstrates using the choice router. It builds upon Example 1-8 to call the GeoNames API only if the latitude property is sent in the request.

Example 1-10. Choice router with expressions

```
<flow name="main">
    <http:inbound-endpoint host="localhost" port="8080"
        path="geonamesproxy" exchange-pattern="request-response" />

    <choice>
        <when expression="#[message.inboundProperties['latitude']] != null]">
```

```
            <http:outbound-endpoint
                address="http://api.geonames.org/findNearbyPOIsOSM
                ?lat=#[message.inboundProperties['latitude']]
                &amp;lng=-122.18&amp;username=demo" method="GET" />
        </when>
    </choice>
</flow>
```

Summary

This chapter has offered a primer on Mule. You have been introduced to some its core features, started your first working Mule application, and connected your first API. But you have merely scratched the surface of Mule, and there are many more features for you to explore. But you're now ready to delve into Mule Cloud/Anypoint Connectors.

CHAPTER 2

Cloud Connectors

As with transports, Cloud Connectors can process messages, communicate with a remote system, and be configured as part of a Mule flow. They can take full advantage of Mule's DSL authoring environment for autocompletion in your favorite IDE or XML editor, offering context-sensitive documentation and access to lists of default and valid values. The main purpose of connectors is to provide you with an easy way to connect to the thousands of APIs out there without having to work with transports or dealing with the different protocols that each API uses. Over the following sections we will start to replace transports with connectors and discuss in detail how to get up and running with some of the most popular APIs.

Installing Cloud Connectors

To get started with Mule Cloud Connect, you will first need to download the connector you want to use. Most Mule modules, such as the HTTP module we used earlier, are prepackaged with Mule and do not require downloading, but you'll have to download and install the Cloud Connectors yourself. Each connector and its associated documentation is available at MuleForge (*http://www.mulesoft.org/muleforge/connectors*), but the steps to download a connector differ slightly depending on your development environment. The following sections detail the most common approaches.

Maven

If you use Apache Maven to build your Mule projects, you can install Cloud Connectors by adding dependency entries for each connector you will be using to your Maven *pom.xml* file. Each connector's documentation page provides you with Maven dependency XML snippets that you can simply copy and paste. To install a connector via Maven, you first need to add the Mule repository to your Maven *pom.xml* file, as shown in Example 2-1.

Example 2-1. Mule repository configuration

```
<repositories>
    <repository>
        <id>mulesoft-releases</id>
        <name>MuleSoft Releases Repository</name>
        <url>http://repository.mulesoft.org/releases/</url>
        <layout>default</layout>
    </repsitory>
</repositories>
```

Once the repository is defined, add a dependency for each connector you want to use—in Example 2-2, it's GeoNames.

Example 2-2. Connector dependency configuration

```
<dependency>
    <groupId>org.mule.modules</groupId>
    <artifactId>mule-module-geonames</artifactId>
    <version>LATEST</version>
</dependency>
```

With your configuration in place, recompiling will download the required connector and its dependencies. After downloading finishes, the connector will be available to your Mule application.

Update Sites

If you are using MuleStudio, you can take advantage of the Cloud Connector's Update site, shown in Figure 2-1.

Use the Update site as follows:

1. Click Help → Install New Software on the Mule menu bar.

2. After the Install window opens, click Add, which is located to the right of the Work with field.

3. Enter the unique name of choice for the update site in the Name field (for example, "Connector Updates").

4. In the Location field, enter **http://repository.mulesoft.org/connectors/ releases/ *3.5.0-cascade***, which points to the Cloud Connector Update site for the current version. In this case *3.5.0-cascade*.

5. A table will appear displaying the available connectors under community and standard categories, the newest version, and the connector name.

6. Click the available version, then click Next, and finally click Finish. The connector will now be available to import into your project.

Figure 2-1. MuleStudio Update site

After following the onscreen instructions, you will be asked to restart your IDE. After that completes, the connector will be available to all your Mule applications.

Manual Installation

If you're not using Maven or Update sites, another option is to download the connector and directly add it to the build path of your project. Each connector hosted on Mule-Forge has a download link that will provide you with the connector of choice as a JAR file.

 Be careful when using this method for installing connectors, as there is no automatic dependency management. If the connector library is reliant on other libraries, which the majority are, you will have to manually add them yourself, which can be time-consuming and error-prone.

If you are using Mule Studio, you can add the connector JAR file and other dependencies to a particular project as follows:

1. Create a *src/main/app/lib* directory in your Studio project.

2. Copy the downloaded JAR file to the *src/main/app/lib* directory.

3. Right click, or select your project and navigate to Project → Properties from the respective menu.

4. Choose Java Build Path from the left-hand menu and then click the Libraries tab in the subsequent view.

5. Click Add JARs..., then use the directory view to navigate through your project and select the JAR files in the *src/main/app/lib* directory.

6. Click OK on the resulting screens to save the changes and go back to your project.

Alternatively, if you're using a stand-alone Mule instance, you can then drop the downloaded connector JAR file into the *lib/user* directory of your Mule distribution.

Namespace and Schema Declarations

The programming model for Mule is XML, and it uses schemas and namespaces to provide a DSL authoring environment. To utilize a connector from a Mule project, you must first include the namespace and schema location declarations within your Mule configuration files.

Each connector's documentation page will provide you with namespace and schema snippets that you can simply copy and paste. Example 2-3 demonstrates the configuration for the namespace and schema locations for the GeoNames connector.

Example 2-3. Connector namespace declarations

```
<?xml version="1.0" encoding="UTF-8"?>
<mule xmlns="http://www.mulesoft.org/schema/mule/core"
      xmlns:spring="http://www.springframework.org/schema/beans"
      xmlns:http="http://www.mulesoft.org/schema/mule/http"
      xmlns:xsi="http://www.w3.org/2001/XMLSchema-instance"
      xmlns:context="http://www.springframework.org/schema/context"
      xmlns:geonames="http://www.mulesoft.org/schema/mule/geonames"
      xsi:schemaLocation="
        http://www.mulesoft.org/schema/mule/core
        http://www.mulesoft.org/schema/mule/core/current/mule.xsd
        http://www.mulesoft.org/schema/mule/http
        http://www.mulesoft.org/schema/mule/http/current/mule-http.xsd
        http://www.mulesoft.org/schema/mule/geonames
        http://www.mulesoft.org/schema/mule/geonames/current/mule-geonames.xsd">
</mule>
```

Global Configuration

After the namespace and schema locations are defined, every Cloud Connector must define a config element. This element is used for setting global service properties such as credentials, security tokens, and API keys. This configuration then applies to all the operations supported by the connector, and once defined, cannot be overridden within a flow.

Each connector's `config` element provides a `name` attribute, which adds an identifier to each configuration so it can be referenced from each connector operation to let Mule know which service configuration to use. Other attributes then differ between each connector. In this case, the GeoNames connector requires that you configure the `user name` attribute that maps to the username parameter of the service:

```xml
<?xml version="1.0" encoding="UTF-8"?>
<mule xmlns="http://www.mulesoft.org/schema/mule/core"
    xmlns:spring="http://www.springframework.org/schema/beans"
    xmlns:http="http://www.mulesoft.org/schema/mule/http"
    xmlns:xsi="http://www.w3.org/2001/XMLSchema-instance"
    xmlns:context="http://www.springframework.org/schema/context"
    xmlns:geonames="http://www.mulesoft.org/schema/mule/geonames"
    xsi:schemaLocation="
        http://www.springframework.org/schema/beans
        http://www.springframework.org/schema/beans/spring-beans-3.0.xsd
        http://www.mulesoft.org/schema/mule/core
        http://www.mulesoft.org/schema/mule/core/current/mule.xsd
        http://www.mulesoft.org/schema/mule/http
        http://www.mulesoft.org/schema/mule/http/current/mule-http.xsd
        http://www.mulesoft.org/schema/mule/geonames
        http://www.mulesoft.org/schema/mule/geonames/current/mule-geonames.xsd">

    <geonames:config username="demo" />

    <flow name="main">
      ...
    </flow>

</mule>
```

As you can see here, we are defining the `config` element within our `mule` configuration, but outside of any `flow`.

Multiple Connector Configurations

Each global `config` element has a `name` attribute and each connector operation has a corresponding `config-ref` attribute that associates the operation with the specific configuration to use. If only one `config` element per connector is present within your app, it is not necessary to explicitly reference a specific configuration, as Mule will default to the only one available. However, if you have multiple configurations per connector, you must explicitly reference the configuration via the `config-ref` attribute on each connector operation.

As you can see from Example 2-4, we have two GeoNames connector configurations. Each of them has a unique `name` attribute that adds an identifier to each configuration.

Underneath the covers, Mule will instantiate two copies of your connector and register them within its registry with the name supplied.

Example 2-4. Referencing connector configurations

```xml
<?xml version="1.0" encoding="UTF-8"?>
<mule xmlns="http://www.mulesoft.org/schema/mule/core"
    xmlns:spring="http://www.springframework.org/schema/beans"
    xmlns:http="http://www.mulesoft.org/schema/mule/http"
    xmlns:xsi="http://www.w3.org/2001/XMLSchema-instance"
    xmlns:context="http://www.springframework.org/schema/context"
    xmlns:geonames="http://www.mulesoft.org/schema/mule/geonames"
    xsi:schemaLocation="
        http://www.springframework.org/schema/beans
        http://www.springframework.org/schema/beans/spring-beans-3.0.xsd
        http://www.mulesoft.org/schema/mule/core
        http://www.mulesoft.org/schema/mule/core/current/mule.xsd
        http://www.mulesoft.org/schema/mule/http
        http://www.mulesoft.org/schema/mule/http/current/mule-http.xsd
        http://www.mulesoft.org/schema/mule/geonames
        http://www.mulesoft.org/schema/mule/geonames/current/mule-geonames.xsd">

    <geonames:config username="demo" name="config1" />

    <geonames:config username="anotherUser" name="config2" />

    <flow name="main">
        <http:inbound-endpoint host="localhost" port="8080"
            path="geonamesproxy" exchange-pattern="request-response" />

        <geonames:find-nearby-pois-osm latitude="37.451" longitude="-122.18"
            config-ref="config1" />

        <geonames:find-nearby-pois-osm latitude="37.451" longitude="-122.18"
            config-ref="config2" />
    </flow>

</mule>
```

Operations are then defined as usual, with the difference that each operation has an attached `config-ref` attribute that will signal the configuration to use it for that particular operation.

Connector Operations

Connector operations wrap up connectivity to external systems or some logic into a simple call that an application can make within its flow. Each operation typically represents a particular API or function that the service provides. Connector operations can be used anywhere in a flow and can be used in a similar way to transports to invoke a remote service:

```
<geonames:find-nearby-pois-osm ... />
```

Each operation is composed of the namespace we previously bound for the connector (`geonames:`) and the operation name (in this case, `find-nearby-pois-osm`). All available operations for a connector are accessible via content assist in your IDE or via the connector's documentation.

Simple Arguments

Instead of using URL query and path parameters, any basic arguments to the API are represented as attributes on the operation that map message payload and properties directly to API arguments. Attributes can be optional or mandatory and can provide content assisted values for enumerations and default values for properties that are not specified.

The following example uses the `find-nearby-pois-osm` operation, which represents the GeoNames Find Nearby Points of Interest API, to find the nearest points of interests for a given lat/lng pair:

```
<geonames:find-nearby-pois-osm latitude="37.451" longitude="-127" />
```

The operation accepts multiple arguments, some required and some optional. The first required arguments, `latitude` and `longitude`, are basic `java.lang.String` parameters that represent the specific coordinates.

Most simple arguments are represented as a `java.lang.String` type, but some arguments that require more specific types, such as `java.util.Date`, need to be constructed as the specific type. Using `java.util.Date` as an example, you may be inclined to configure a date argument as follows, which would lead to an error:

```
<someconnector:operation date="1984-06-03" />
```

This configuration would pass the date to the connector as a `String`, when the connector needs a `java.util.Date` type. The correct way to map the date value to the argument is to generate a `java.util.Date` object. One convenient way is to use the `groovy` expression evaluator, like so:

```
<someconnector:operation
    date="#[groovy:Date.parse("yyyy-MM-dd", "1984-06-03")]" />
```

The same also goes for `boolean` values. If you need to pass in a `boolean` value, construct it as the correct type using a `groovy` expression again:

```
<someconnector:operation true-or-false="#[groovy:true]" />
```

Information on each argument's type can be found at the connector's documentation page online and also as part of content assist. Connectors and the DevKit have support for the following types:

- `int`
- `float`
- `long`
- `byte`
- `short`
- `double`
- `boolean`
- `char`
- `java.lang.Integer`
- `java.lang.Float`
- `java.lang.Long`
- `java.lang.Byte`
- `java.lang.Short`
- `java.lang.Double`
- `java.lang.Boolean`
- `java.lang.Character`
- `java.lang.String`
- `java.math.BigDecimal`
- `java.math.BigInteger`
- `java.util.Date`
- `java.lang.Class`
- `java.net.URL`
- `java.net.URI`

Collections and Structured Arguments

Complex types

More complex arguments, such as collections or structured objects that can't really be expressed as simple attributes, can instead be represented as complex types as child elements within the operation itself. Example 2-5 demonstrates using the GeoNames `astergdem` operation, which accepts a set of lists for latitudes and longitudes as input.

Example 2-5. Collections configuration

```
<geonames:astergdem>
    <geonames:latitudes>
        <geonames:latitude>37.451</geonames:latitude>
        <geonames:latitude>37.450</geonames:latitude>
    </geonames:latitudes>
    <geonames:longitudes>
        <geonames:longitude>-122.18</geonames:longitude>
        <geonames:longitude>-122.18</geonames:longitude>
    </geonames:longitudes>
</geonames:astergdem>
```

The example first defines the root element for each list (for example, `geonames:lati` `tudes`). Secondly, the list's root element contains an array of child elements representing the list items (for example, `geonames:latitude`).

As with collections, any complex types such as custom Java classes can be passed to the operation via child elements. Let's take a look at the following example from the Get-Satisfaction connector. One of the connectors operations, `getsatisfaction:create-topic-at-company`, has a method signature that requires a custom Java class: `org.mule.module.getsatisfaction.model.Topic`. Inspecting this class you will see that it's a simple POJO with some fields for subject, content, products, etc., similar to the following snippet:

```
public class Topic extends Post {
    ...
    private String subject;
    private String content;
    private Style style;
    private List<Product> products;
    private List<String> keywords;
    ...
}
```

Any custom classes like this are automatically deconstructed and reconstructed as complex types within the schemas themselves, enabling them to be defined easily as child elements of the operation.

As you can see in Example 2-6, the topic class is now constructed directly using XML via the `getsatisfaction:topic` element. Any simple properties of the class (as documented in the earlier list of supported types) are represented as normal (attributes on the element directly), such as `subject`, `content`, and `style`. And any complex properties such as custom classes and collections are represented as further nested complex types within the element, as demonstrated by the `getsatisfaction:product` property.

Example 2-6. Complex type configuration

```
<getsatisfaction:create-topic-at-company companyId="mulesoft">
    <getsatisfaction:topic
        subject="test for product affiliate"
        content="additional detail goes here"
        style="PRAISE">
        <getsatisfaction:products>
            <getsatisfaction:product name="muleion"/>
        </getsatisfaction:products>
        <getsatisfaction:keywords>
            <getsatisfaction:keyword>keyword</getsatisfaction:keyword>
        </getsatisfaction:keywords>
    </getsatisfaction:topic>
</getsatisfaction:create-topic-at-company>
```

Passing by reference

For everything else that is not in the supported list of types, the DevKit allows the information to be passed along using references. As we saw in Example 2-5 and Example 2-6, we can build up our objects using the strongly typed schemas that represent the object itself. However, in previous versions of the DevKit, this wasn't possible, and even now you may want to reference an object or collection already constructed elsewhere. To allow this, connector operations that require structured arguments also allow you to reference preconstructed arguments via an attribute on the child element named `ref`.

Using the Collections example in Example 2-5, we can instead build our list outside of our operation and refer to it as follows:

```
<spring:bean id="latitudeA" class="java.lang.String">
    <spring:constructor-arg value="37.451" />
</spring:bean>

<spring:bean id="latitudeB" class="java.lang.String">
    <spring:constructor-arg value="37.451" />
</spring:bean>

<spring:bean id="list"
    class="org.springframework.beans.factory.config.ListFactoryBean">
    <spring:property name="sourceList">
        <spring:list>
            <spring:ref bean="latitudeA" />
            <spring:ref bean="latitudeB" />
        </spring:list>
    </spring:property>
</spring:bean>

...

<geonames:astergdem>
```

```
...
    <geonames:latitudes ref="list" />
    ...
</geonames:astergdem>
```

This example uses spring to manually build our list from two Strings and then reference the list from a ref attribute using the id of the spring:bean (in this case, list).

The same functionality we've shown for collections can be applied to custom classes. Using the complex type example in Example 2-6, we can instead build the object outside of the operation and then reference it as follows:

```
<spring:bean id="keywordA" class="java.lang.String">
    <spring:constructor-arg value="muleion" />
</spring:bean>

<spring:bean id="product" class="org.mule.module.getsatisfaction.model.Product">
    <spring:constructor-arg value="muleion" />
</spring:bean>

<spring:bean id="keywords" class="org.springframework.beans.factory.config.
                            ListFactoryBean">
    <spring:property name="sourceList">
        <spring:list>
            <spring:ref bean="keywordA"/>
        </spring:list>
    </spring:property>
</spring:bean>


<spring:bean id="topic"
    class="org.mule.module.getsatisfaction.model.Topic">
    <spring:property name="subject" value="test for product affiliate" />
    <spring:property name="content" value="additional detail goes here" />
    <spring:property name="keywords" ref="keywords" />
    <spring:property name="product" ref="product" />
</spring:bean>

...

<getsatisfaction:create-topic-at-company companyId="mulesoft">
    <getsatisfaction:topic ref="topic" />
</getsatisfaction:create-topic-at-company>
```

This example uses spring to manually build our org.mule.module.getsatisfaction.model.Topic object and then reference it from the ref attribute using the id of the spring:bean (in this case, topic).

Expression Evaluation

Previous examples use static values as inputs to operation arguments, but in real life you will probably want to use variable values extracted from requests, responses, or properties files. To support this, each connector operation can handle full expression evaluation and argument transformation as shown in "Variables and Expressions" on page 8.

The expression evaluation performed by Example 2-7 allows us to parameterize values to operations from a variety of sources. This example uses the MEL to extract the parameters from the header of an incoming HTTP request, but if the source of the message is XML, JSON, or pretty much anything, there's an expression evaluator for it. More information on expressions can be found here (*http://bit.ly/1nfAsgD*).

Example 2-7. Connector operation with expressions

```
<geonames:find-nearby-pois-osm
    latitude="#[message.inboundProperties['latitude']]"
    longitude="#[message.inboundProperties['longitude']]" />
```

Parsing the Response

The response format from each operation can differ between connectors. Some connectors provide the raw response from the service provider's API whereas other will provide a bound Java object representing the response. Take GeoNames for example. GeoNames offers both XML and JSON formatted responses. The configuration in Example 1-4 would result in the operation returning the default response format, XML. Once invoked, it will return an XML response similar to the following:

```
<?xml version="1.0" encoding="UTF-8"?>
<geonames>
    <poi>
        <name>Cook's Seafood</name>
        <typeClass>amenity</typeClass>
        <typeName>restaurant</typeName>
        <lng>-122.1795529</lng>
        <lat>37.4516093</lat>
        <distance>0.08</distance>
    </poi>
    <poi>
        <name>Starbucks</name>
        <typeClass>amenity</typeClass>
        <typeName>cafe</typeName>
        <lng>-122.1803386</lng>
        <lat>37.452055</lat>
        <distance>0.12</distance>
    </poi>
    <poi>
        <name>Safeway</name>
        <typeClass>shop</typeClass>
```

```
        <typeName>supermarket</typeName>
        <lng>-122.1787081</lng>
        <lat>37.4507461</lat>
        <distance>0.12</distance>
    </poi>
    <poi>
        <name>Akasaka</name>
        <typeClass>amenity</typeClass>
        <typeName>restaurant</typeName>
        <lng>-122.1809239</lng>
        <lat>37.4524367</lat>
        <distance>0.18</distance>
    </poi>
</geonames>
```

The GeoNames connector allows you to switch between the available response formats by specifying an optional argument either on the operation itself or via the connector's config element. In the case of the GeoNames connector, you can specify the argument at the operation level through the attribute named type:

```
<geonames:find-nearby-pois-osm latitude="37.51"
        longitude="-122.18" type="json"/>
```

Here we have added the optional type argument and set it's value to json. With this new configuration in place, instead of seeing XML, you should now see a JSON-formatted response, similar to Example 2-8.

Example 2-8. GeoNames JSON sample response

```
{"poi":[
    {"typeName":"restaurant","distance":"0.08","name":"Cook's Seafood",
        "lng":"-122.1795529","typeClass":"amenity","lat":"37.4516093"},
    {"typeName":"cafe","distance":"0.12","name":"Starbucks",
        "lng":"-122.1803386","typeClass":"amenity","lat":"37.452055"},
    {"typeName":"fire_hydrant","distance":"0.14","name":"",
        "lng":"-122.1784682","typeClass":"amenity","lat":"37.4510495"},
    {"typeName":"fire_hydrant","distance":"0.19","name":"",
        "lng":"-122.1800146","typeClass":"amenity","lat":"37.4493291"},
    {"typeName":"restaurant","distance":"0.18","name":"Akasaka",
        "lng":"-122.1809239","typeClass":"amenity","lat":"37.4524367"},
    {"typeName":"fast_food","distance":"0.16","name":"Rubios",
        "lng":"-122.1784509","typeClass":"amenity","lat":"37.4501701"},
    {"typeName":"cinema","distance":"0.21","name":"Guild",
        "lng":"-122.1812488","typeClass":"amenity","lat":"37.4525935"},
    {"typeName":"cafe","distance":"0.22","name":"Pete's Coffee",
        "lng":"-122.1780217","typeClass":"amenity","lat":"37.4498336"},
    {"typeName":"fast_food","distance":"0.23","name":"Applewood2Go",
        "lng":"-122.1816743","typeClass":"amenity","lat":"37.4526078"},
    {"typeName":"fire_hydrant","distance":"0.23","name":"",
        "lng":"-122.178034","typeClass":"amenity","lat":"37.449606"}
]}
```

If you are unsure what response formats are available, or at what level they are configured, they can be found by using content assist or by reading the connector documentation. Additional information on particular responses can also be found using the service provider's documentation.

Summary

In summary, connectors make the simple tasks easy and the hard tasks possible by taking a step back from HTTP and protocols to provide a higher level of abstraction and a consistent interaction model with APIs, allowing developers to concentrate on the task at hand.

The examples in this chapter have concentrated on working with a single service in silo. But more than likely, you'll want to compose applications that span a multitude of services and data formats. The upcoming chapters will take a look at some of the core components of Mule to start building real life integration applications.

CHAPTER 3

Orchestrating Cloud Connectors

Application or service orchestration is the process of integrating two or more applications and/or services together to automate a process, or synchronize data in real time. Orchestration provides an approach to integration that decouples applications from each other and provides capabilities for message routing, security, transformation, and reliability. So far, we have been looking at connectors in silos. But typically you'll want to compose applications that span a multitude of services, such as cloud to cloud and cloud to on-premise systems. Although cloud services bring new challenges to integration, some things never change, and *Enterprise Integration Patterns* (EIP) principles are still as valid as ever. Alongside cloud connectivity, Mule's solid roots in EIP give you a wealth of tools to route and transform data efficiently and reliably between systems.

Transforming Data with Mule

As discussed at the beginning of this book, there are a multitude of protocols when it comes to working with APIs as well as a plethora of data interchange formats. No doubt you will need to transform data between services from XML to JSON and vice versa, from bound response objects to a serialized form, or even from external data to your own internal canonical data format.

To accomplish these changes, Mule comes with a vast array of transformers out of the box to help you work with various different data formats. It also allows you to implement your own via custom Java classes or MEL expressions. Here we will attempt to cover the basics of transformation and look at some specialized transformers to work with some of the most common formats.

Working with Transformers

Transformers are an implementation of the EIP Message Translator pattern (*http:// bit.ly/1nfAx3T*). It simply translates a message from one format to another.

Transformers in Mule are message processors that modify the payload and/or properties of a message. We have already seen some basic transformation techniques in Chapter 1 using the set-payload and set-property message processors. These are basic in the sense that they simply overwrite or create the payload or message property. Mule also has an array of transformers for more specialized scenarios such as serializing or compressing data. A more detailed list of available transformers can be found in the Transformers documentation (*http://bit.ly/1nfAzZy*). To demonstrate some more advanced transformation, we will look at how we can work with the popular JSON format.

Working with JSON

JSON is a standard based on a subset of the JavaScript syntax to simply and effectively describe an object. Over the last few years, JSON has taken the mantle as the de facto data interchange format among APIs; most API providers choose it as their default and some even exclusively as their data interchange format. JSON is favored by many because it is smaller and lighter than traditional formats such as XML—an important factor when building mobile applications, for example.

Whatever the reason for JSON's rise to fame, we need a way to transform and embrace these curly braces. Mule has excellent support for JSON and allows you to query, transform, and marshal JSON documents with ease. In this section we will have a look at these features and see how we can work with some popular JSON APIs.

Transforming JSON. Mule allows you to easily transform JSON by serializing and deserializing JSON using the popular Jackson framework (*http://jackson.codehaus.org/*). Similar to JAXB for XML, we can annotate a Java class for binding JSON values to specific object properties. Using the sample JSON returned from GeoNames in Example 2-8, we can build a simple Java representation of the GeoNames response:

```
package org.oreilly.mulecloud;

import org.codehaus.jackson.annotate.JsonAutoDetect;

@JsonAutoDetect
public class GeonamesResponse {
    private List<POI> poi;

    // getters and setters omitted for brevity
}

package org.oreilly.mulecloud;

import org.codehaus.jackson.annotate.JsonAutoDetect;

@JsonAutoDetect
public class POI {
    private String typeName;
    private String distance;
```

```
    private String name;
    private String lng;
    private String typeClass;
    private String lat;

    // getters and setters omitted for brevity
}
```

As you can see, these are just standard POJOs annotated with @JsonAutoDetect. This annotation, provided by Jackson, will automatically detect getters and setters for each property based on the name and type of the equivalent JSON property and will set their values accordingly. Jackson provides a wide range of annotations and tools for more complex mapping. More information can be found from the Jackson documentation (*http://jackson.codehaus.org/*). Example 3-1 demonstrates how we can transform our GeoNames response into our Java object.

Example 3-1. Deserializing JSON

```
<?xml version="1.0" encoding="UTF-8"?>
<mule xmlns="http://www.mulesoft.org/schema/mule/core"
    xmlns:spring="http://www.springframework.org/schema/beans"
    xmlns:http="http://www.mulesoft.org/schema/mule/http"
    xmlns:json="http://www.mulesoft.org/schema/mule/json"
    xmlns:xsi="http://www.w3.org/2001/XMLSchema-instance"
    xmlns:context="http://www.springframework.org/schema/context"
    xmlns:geonames="http://www.mulesoft.org/schema/mule/geonames"
    xsi:schemaLocation="
        http://www.springframework.org/schema/beans
        http://www.springframework.org/schema/beans/spring-beans-3.0.xsd
        http://www.mulesoft.org/schema/mule/core
        http://www.mulesoft.org/schema/mule/core/current/mule.xsd
        http://www.mulesoft.org/schema/mule/http
        http://www.mulesoft.org/schema/mule/http/current/mule-http.xsd
        http://www.mulesoft.org/schema/mule/json
        http://www.mulesoft.org/schema/mule/json/current/mule-json.xsd
        http://www.mulesoft.org/schema/mule/geonames
        http://www.mulesoft.org/schema/mule/geonames/current/mule-geonames.xsd">

    <geonames:config username="demo" name="geonames" />

    <flow name="main">
        <http:inbound-endpoint host="localhost" port="8080"
            path="geonamesproxy" exchange-pattern="request-response" />

        <geonames:find-nearby-pois-osm latitude="37.451" longitude="-122.18"
            config-ref="geonames" type="json" />

        <json:json-to-object-transformer
            returnClass="org.oreilly.mulecloud.GeonamesResponse" />

        <logger message="#[payload]" level="INFO" />
```

```
    </flow>

</mule>
```

As you can see, it is a simple matter of changing the `returnClass` attribute to our own class definition. Most transformers will provide this sometimes optional attribute as well as others such as `encoding` to set what encoding the returned data should use. There will also be specific attributes for specific transformers, which can be found in the transformers documentation or via content-assist.

Specific transformers such as the JSON ones usually come in pairs, with the second being able to undo and reverse the actions of the first. So just as we deserialized our JSON to a Java object, we can also serialize an object back to JSON via its alter ego: the `object-to-json-transformer` (see Example 3-2).

Example 3-2. Serializing JSON

```
<?xml version="1.0" encoding="UTF-8"?>
<mule xmlns="http://www.mulesoft.org/schema/mule/core"
    xmlns:spring="http://www.springframework.org/schema/beans"
    xmlns:http="http://www.mulesoft.org/schema/mule/http"
    xmlns:json="http://www.mulesoft.org/schema/mule/json"
    xmlns:xsi="http://www.w3.org/2001/XMLSchema-instance"
    xmlns:context="http://www.springframework.org/schema/context"
    xmlns:geonames="http://www.mulesoft.org/schema/mule/geonames"
    xsi:schemaLocation="
        http://www.springframework.org/schema/beans
        http://www.springframework.org/schema/beans/spring-beans-3.0.xsd
        http://www.mulesoft.org/schema/mule/core
        http://www.mulesoft.org/schema/mule/core/current/mule.xsd
        http://www.mulesoft.org/schema/mule/http
        http://www.mulesoft.org/schema/mule/http/current/mule-http.xsd
        http://www.mulesoft.org/schema/mule/json
        http://www.mulesoft.org/schema/mule/json/current/mule-json.xsd
        http://www.mulesoft.org/schema/mule/geonames
        http://www.mulesoft.org/schema/mule/geonames/current/mule-geonames.xsd">

    <geonames:config username="demo" name="geonames" />

    <flow name="main">
        <http:inbound-endpoint host="localhost" port="8080"
            path="geonamesproxy" exchange-pattern="request-response" />

        <geonames:find-nearby-pois-osm latitude="37.451" longitude="-122.18"
            config-ref="geonames" type="json" />

        <json:json-to-object-transformer
            returnClass="org.oreilly.mulecloud.GeonamesResponse" />

        <json:object-to-json-transformer />
```

```
        <logger message="#[payload]" level="INFO" />
    </flow>

</mule>
```

Querying JSON. As we have seen, MEL provides an easy-to-use `xpath` function for querying XML documents. Unfortunately, MEL does not provide an equivalent for JSON. There is a deprecated `json` expression evaluator, but Mule now favors a combination of JSON transformers and standard MEL expressions. Although this approach does not have all the features of XPath, JSON documents tend to be much simpler and this technique should cover most use cases. Example 3-3 demonstrates how we can query the JSON returned from GeoNames.

Example 3-3. Querying JSON

```
<?xml version="1.0" encoding="UTF-8"?>
<mule xmlns="http://www.mulesoft.org/schema/mule/core"
    xmlns:spring="http://www.springframework.org/schema/beans"
    xmlns:http="http://www.mulesoft.org/schema/mule/http"
    xmlns:json="http://www.mulesoft.org/schema/mule/json"
    xmlns:xsi="http://www.w3.org/2001/XMLSchema-instance"
    xmlns:context="http://www.springframework.org/schema/context"
    xmlns:geonames="http://www.mulesoft.org/schema/mule/geonames"
    xsi:schemaLocation="
        http://www.springframework.org/schema/beans
        http://www.springframework.org/schema/beans/spring-beans-3.0.xsd
        http://www.mulesoft.org/schema/mule/core
        http://www.mulesoft.org/schema/mule/core/current/mule.xsd
        http://www.mulesoft.org/schema/mule/http
        http://www.mulesoft.org/schema/mule/http/current/mule-http.xsd
        http://www.mulesoft.org/schema/mule/json
        http://www.mulesoft.org/schema/mule/json/current/mule-json.xsd
        http://www.mulesoft.org/schema/mule/geonames
        http://www.mulesoft.org/schema/mule/geonames/current/mule-geonames.xsd">

    <geonames:config username="demo" name="geonames" />

    <flow name="main">
        <http:inbound-endpoint host="localhost" port="8080"
            path="geonamesproxy" exchange-pattern="request-response" />

        <geonames:find-nearby-pois-osm latitude="37.451" longitude="-122.18"
            config-ref="geonames" type="json" />

        <json:json-to-object-transformer returnClass="java.util.HashMap" />

          <expression-transformer expression="#[payload.poi]" />

        <logger message="#[payload]" level="INFO" />
    </flow>
```

```
</mule>
```

To get the JSON response into something we can easily work with using MEL, we transform the response to a Map implementation, using the `json:json-to-object-transformer` passing in the `returnClass` as a `java.util.HashMap`. JSON documents convert easily into a Map implementation as they are just a set of key/value pairs. The map key will represent the object's property name and the value will represent the properties value. Nested objects will in turn be represented as a Map of Map's recursively.

Once transformed to a Map, we can easily query it using standard MEL operations (i.e., `#[payload.poi]`, where `poi` is the key to the map and the value will be a list of POIs).

To query individual list entries, we can also use standard MEL syntax passing in the array pointer of the entry we want:

```
<expression-transformer expression="#[payload.poi[0].name]" />
```

This will now produce a single POI entry as follows:

```
INFO     2013-09-21     15:34:25,350     [[geonames].geonamesFlow1.stage1.02]
org.mule.api.processor.LoggerMessageProcessor: Cook's Seafood
```

Here we have introduced another transformer, `expression-transformer`, which will transform the payload into the result of the expression—in this case, the `name` property of the point of interest.

Routing Data with Mule

Mule has always had support for many routing options. Routers in Mule implement various Enterprise Integration Patterns. They are message processors that determine how messages are directed within a flow. Alongside MEL, routers can decide on a course of action based on the contents, properties, or context of a message. There are many different routing options available within Mule and a comprehensive list can be found in the Routing Message Processors documentation (*http://bit.ly/1nfAF3D*). Let's see how we can implement some different routing techniques within our application.

Working with Collections

As there is probably always more than one point of interest for any given place in the world, we need a way to work with collections of results. Mule supports multiple ways of working with collections from traditional EIP `splitters` to additional routers such as `foreach`, which most programmers of any language will be familiar with. Let's first look at the `splitter`.

Splitting things up

As the name suggests, a `splitter` can split the current message into its individual parts. It can do this via a custom MEL expression, or it can simply split the elements of a standard Java collection. Continuing our previous example, we have a list of points of interest represented by a Java Collection of `org.oreilly.mulecloud.POI` objects. Example 3-4 demonstrates how we can split the collection into individual points.

Example 3-4. Splitting things up

```
<?xml version="1.0" encoding="UTF-8"?>
<mule xmlns="http://www.mulesoft.org/schema/mule/core"
    xmlns:spring="http://www.springframework.org/schema/beans"
    xmlns:http="http://www.mulesoft.org/schema/mule/http"
    xmlns:json="http://www.mulesoft.org/schema/mule/json"
    xmlns:xsi="http://www.w3.org/2001/XMLSchema-instance"
    xmlns:context="http://www.springframework.org/schema/context"
    xmlns:geonames="http://www.mulesoft.org/schema/mule/geonames"
    xsi:schemaLocation="
        http://www.springframework.org/schema/beans
        http://www.springframework.org/schema/beans/spring-beans-3.0.xsd
        http://www.mulesoft.org/schema/mule/core
        http://www.mulesoft.org/schema/mule/core/current/mule.xsd
        http://www.mulesoft.org/schema/mule/http
        http://www.mulesoft.org/schema/mule/http/current/mule-http.xsd
        http://www.mulesoft.org/schema/mule/json
        http://www.mulesoft.org/schema/mule/json/current/mule-json.xsd
        http://www.mulesoft.org/schema/mule/geonames
        http://www.mulesoft.org/schema/mule/geonames/current/mule-geonames.xsd">

    <geonames:config username="demo" name="geonames" />

    <flow name="main">
        <http:inbound-endpoint host="localhost" port="8080"
                path="geonamesproxy" exchange-pattern="request-response" />

         <geonames:find-nearby-pois-osm latitude="37.451" longitude="-122.18"
             config-ref="geonames" type="json" />

        <json:json-to-object-transformer
            returnClass="org.oreilly.mulecloud.GeonamesResponse" />

        <splitter expression="#[payload.poi]" />

        <logger message="#[payload.name]" level="INFO" />
    </flow>

</mule>
```

In the previous example, we split the collection of POIs using the `splitter` message processor, passing in the MEL expression `#[payload.poi]`: `payload` is the part of the message we want to query and poi is the property name on our object containing the collection of POIs.

With the payload split into its individual entries, the application will run each subsequent message processor once per POI. As we are logging the name of the POI, we should be able to see individual logger output for each POI similar to the following:

```
INFO     2013-09-21     15:34:25,350     [[geonames].geonamesFlow1.stage1.02]
org.mule.api.processor.LoggerMessageProcessor:  Cook's Seafood
INFO     2013-09-21     15:34:25,350     [[geonames].geonamesFlow1.stage1.02]
org.mule.api.processor.LoggerMessageProcessor:  Starbucks
INFO     2013-09-21     15:34:25,350     [[geonames].geonamesFlow1.stage1.02]
org.mule.api.processor.LoggerMessageProcessor:  Akaska
```

The traditional foreach

The foreach router should sound familiar to any developer, regardless of his technology background. In short, it iterates a collection and can perform an action "for each" entry in the collection. Using the same collection as the previous example, Example 3-5 demonstrates how we can iterate the collection instead of splitting it up.

Example 3-5. Iterating the collection

```
<?xml version="1.0" encoding="UTF-8"?>
<mule xmlns="http://www.mulesoft.org/schema/mule/core"
    xmlns:spring="http://www.springframework.org/schema/beans"
    xmlns:http="http://www.mulesoft.org/schema/mule/http"
    xmlns:json="http://www.mulesoft.org/schema/mule/json"
    xmlns:xsi="http://www.w3.org/2001/XMLSchema-instance"
    xmlns:context="http://www.springframework.org/schema/context"
    xmlns:geonames="http://www.mulesoft.org/schema/mule/geonames"
    xsi:schemaLocation="
        http://www.springframework.org/schema/beans
        http://www.springframework.org/schema/beans/spring-beans-3.0.xsd
        http://www.mulesoft.org/schema/mule/core
        http://www.mulesoft.org/schema/mule/core/current/mule.xsd
        http://www.mulesoft.org/schema/mule/http
        http://www.mulesoft.org/schema/mule/http/current/mule-http.xsd
        http://www.mulesoft.org/schema/mule/json
        http://www.mulesoft.org/schema/mule/json/current/mule-json.xsd
        http://www.mulesoft.org/schema/mule/geonames
        http://www.mulesoft.org/schema/mule/geonames/current/mule-geonames.xsd">

    <geonames:config username="demo" name="geonames" />

    <flow name="main">
        <http:inbound-endpoint host="localhost" port="8080"
            path="geonamesproxy" exchange-pattern="request-response" />

        <geonames:find-nearby-pois-osm latitude="37.451" longitude="-122.18"
            config-ref="geonames" type="json" />
```

```
<json:json-to-object-transformer
    returnClass="org.oreilly.mulecloud.GeonamesResponse" />

<foreach collection="#[payload.poi]">
    <logger message="#[payload.name]" level="INFO" />
</foreach>

</flow>

</mule>
```

In the previous example, we just need to pass the `foreach` router the collection we want
to iterate. As in the previous example, we use the collection of POIs passing in the MEL
expression `#[payload.poi]`: `payload` is the part of the message we want to query and
`poi` is the property name on our object containing the collection of POIs.

Conditional Routing

No application has a catch-all policy and no doubt you will want to conditionally decide
where your data goes and when. The typical "if this, then that" is familiar to any developer from any language and integration applications are no exception. First, let's look
at the `choice` router.

The choice router

Alongside MEL, the `choice` router can decide on a course of action based on the contents, properties, or context of a message. Example 3-6 demonstrates using the `choice`
router. It builds upon Example 3-4 to log the name of the point of interest, only if the
`typeName` property is of type "cafe." Otherwise it will log "No coffee here." This example
is a simple if/else route. The `choice` route also allows you to specify as many `when` blocks
as you want for more complex routing.

Example 3-6. The choice router

```
<?xml version="1.0" encoding="UTF-8"?>
<mule xmlns="http://www.mulesoft.org/schema/mule/core"
    xmlns:spring="http://www.springframework.org/schema/beans"
    xmlns:http="http://www.mulesoft.org/schema/mule/http"
    xmlns:json="http://www.mulesoft.org/schema/mule/json"
    xmlns:xsi="http://www.w3.org/2001/XMLSchema-instance"
    xmlns:context="http://www.springframework.org/schema/context"
    xmlns:geonames="http://www.mulesoft.org/schema/mule/geonames"
    xsi:schemaLocation="
        http://www.springframework.org/schema/beans
        http://www.springframework.org/schema/beans/spring-beans-3.0.xsd
        http://www.mulesoft.org/schema/mule/core
        http://www.mulesoft.org/schema/mule/core/current/mule.xsd
        http://www.mulesoft.org/schema/mule/http
        http://www.mulesoft.org/schema/mule/http/current/mule-http.xsd
```

```
        http://www.mulesoft.org/schema/mule/json
        http://www.mulesoft.org/schema/mule/json/current/mule-json.xsd
        http://www.mulesoft.org/schema/mule/geonames
        http://www.mulesoft.org/schema/mule/geonames/current/mule-geonames.xsd">

    <geonames:config username="demo" name="geonames" />

    <flow name="main">
        <http:inbound-endpoint host="localhost" port="8080"
            path="geonamesproxy" exchange-pattern="request-response" />

        <geonames:find-nearby-pois-osm latitude="37.451" longitude="-122.18"
            config-ref="geonames" type="json" />

        <json:json-to-object-transformer
            returnClass="org.oreilly.mulecloud.GeonamesResponse" />

        <splitter expression="#[payload.poi]" />

        <choice>
            <when expression="#[payload.typeName == 'cafe']">
                <logger message="#[payload.name]" level="INFO" />
            </when>
        </choice>
    </flow>

</mule>
```

Filtering

In contrast to the choice router, filters in Mule are designed to simply drop messages that do not meet your conditions rather than giving you an alternative route. There are many preconfigured filters in Mule, such as the idempotent-filter for filtering unique messages, and even more specific ones, such as the schema-validation-filter for filtering only valid XML documents. A comprehensive list of available filters can be found at *http://bit.ly/1nfAKnR*. You can also create your own filters via implementing Mule's Filter (*http://bit.ly/1nfAPrG*) interface or via MEL expressions using the expression-filter. Example 3-7 demonstrates using the simple MEL expressions to filter unwanted messages.

Example 3-7. Filters

```
<?xml version="1.0" encoding="UTF-8"?>
<mule xmlns="http://www.mulesoft.org/schema/mule/core"
    xmlns:spring="http://www.springframework.org/schema/beans"
    xmlns:http="http://www.mulesoft.org/schema/mule/http"
    xmlns:json="http://www.mulesoft.org/schema/mule/json"
    xmlns:xsi="http://www.w3.org/2001/XMLSchema-instance"
    xmlns:context="http://www.springframework.org/schema/context"
    xmlns:geonames="http://www.mulesoft.org/schema/mule/geonames"
    xsi:schemaLocation="
```

```
            http://www.springframework.org/schema/beans
            http://www.springframework.org/schema/beans/spring-beans-3.0.xsd
            http://www.mulesoft.org/schema/mule/core
            http://www.mulesoft.org/schema/mule/core/current/mule.xsd
            http://www.mulesoft.org/schema/mule/http
            http://www.mulesoft.org/schema/mule/http/current/mule-http.xsd
            http://www.mulesoft.org/schema/mule/json
            http://www.mulesoft.org/schema/mule/json/current/mule-json.xsd
            http://www.mulesoft.org/schema/mule/geonames
            http://www.mulesoft.org/schema/mule/geonames/current/mule-geonames.xsd">

    <geonames:config username="demo" name="geonames" />

    <flow name="main">
        <http:inbound-endpoint host="localhost" port="8080"
            path="geonamesproxy" exchange-pattern="request-response" />

        <geonames:find-nearby-pois-osm latitude="37.451" longitude="-122.18"
            config-ref="geonames" type="json" />;

        <json:json-to-object-transformer
            returnClass="org.oreilly.mulecloud.GeonamesResponse" />

        <splitter expression="#[payload.poi]" />

        <expression-filter expression="#[payload.typeName == 'cafe']" />

        <logger message="#[payload.name]" level="INFO" />
    </flow>

</mule>
```

Just as with the choice router, the expression-filter can filter messages based on the contents, properties, or context of a message. This example will log the name of the point of interest, only if the typeName property is of type "cafe." Otherwise, the point of interest will simply be ignored.

Unwanted Messages

Although unwanted messages appear to be lost forever, there is an option of routing the unwanted entries to a dead letter channel for alternative processing. This can be done by wrapping your filter within the `message-filter` and setting its `onUnaccepted` attribute to define where to send the message. This can be another flow or message processor, referenced by name:

```
<flow name="main">
  <message-filter onUnaccepted="unwantedMessages">
    <expression-filter expression="#[payload.typeName ==
'cafe']" />
  </message-filter>
</flow>

<flow name="unwantedMessages">
  <logger message="Unwanted: #[payload.name]" level="INFO" />
</flow>
```

Reliable Routing

However much third-party APIs are abstracted away, they are still a third-party dependency on your application and, by their nature, outside of your control. You typically don't see API juggernauts like Twitter or Salesforce go down, but it does happen and depending on the API provider, sometimes a lot.

Those with a background in messaging protocols such as JMS will be familiar with reliable and guaranteed delivery. However, since most APIs are web APIs, they are understandably built on top of HTTP, which doesn't afford such luxuries.

Fortunately, Mule provides routers that can build resiliency and reliability into your API integrations. Let's start by taking a look at the `first-successful` router.

The first-successful router

The `first-successful`, as the name may suggest, will route a message to a group of message processors until one succeeds. After the "first" operation completes successfully, any further message processors are ignored.

Example 3-8 demonstrates calling two GeoNames operations until one of them succeeds. First, Mule will try to request a list of nearby points of interest via the `find-nearby-pois-osm` operation. If it fails, Mule will move on to the second operation and attempt to request a nearby placename via the `find-nearby-place-name` operation. This list can have as many operations as you want and will execute each one sequentially until one succeeds. One useful situation for this could be when you have multiple API providers providing the same or similar service (for example, a bookstore where you can try requesting a price from Amazon and, if it fails, you could fall back to Google Books, and so on).

Example 3-8. The first-successful router

```xml
<?xml version="1.0" encoding="UTF-8"?>
<mule xmlns="http://www.mulesoft.org/schema/mule/core"
   xmlns:spring="http://www.springframework.org/schema/beans"
   xmlns:http="http://www.mulesoft.org/schema/mule/http"
   xmlns:xsi="http://www.w3.org/2001/XMLSchema-instance"
   xmlns:context="http://www.springframework.org/schema/context"
   xmlns:geonames="http://www.mulesoft.org/schema/mule/geonames"
   xsi:schemaLocation="
       http://www.springframework.org/schema/beans
       http://www.springframework.org/schema/beans/spring-beans-3.0.xsd
       http://www.mulesoft.org/schema/mule/core
       http://www.mulesoft.org/schema/mule/core/current/mule.xsd
       http://www.mulesoft.org/schema/mule/http
       http://www.mulesoft.org/schema/mule/http/current/mule-http.xsd
       http://www.mulesoft.org/schema/mule/geonames
       http://www.mulesoft.org/schema/mule/geonames/current/mule-geonames.xsd">

    <geonames:config username="demo" name="geonames" />

    <flow name="main">
        <http:inbound-endpoint host="localhost" port="8080"
            path="geonamesproxy" exchange-pattern="request-response" />

        <first-successful>
           <geonames:find-nearby-pois-osm latitude="37.451" longitude="-122.18"
               config-ref="geonames" />
           <geonames:find-nearby-place-name latitude="37.451" longitude="-122.18"
               config-ref="geonames" />
        </first-successful>

        <logger message="#[payload]" level="INFO" />
    </flow>

</mule>
```

The until-successful router

In contrast to the `first-successful` router, the `until-successful` router allows you to repeat a single operation until its deemed successful. Until the message processor succeeds, it will be retried over and over depending on your configuration.

The `until-successful` router is basically an implementation of the store-and-forward pattern. It stores the original message within an object store and forwards it to the message processor encapsulated within the router until the result is deemed successful. Example 3-9 demonstrates attempting to call the GeoNames `find-nearby-pois-osm` operation a possible five times until it succeeds. In this example, we define a simple in-memory object store to store the original message. The `maxRetries` attribute defines the maximum amount of retries and works alongside the `secondsBetweenRetires` attribute to configure how long to wait between each attempt.

Example 3-9. The until-successful router

```xml
<?xml version="1.0" encoding="UTF-8"?>
<mule xmlns="http://www.mulesoft.org/schema/mule/core"
    xmlns:spring="http://www.springframework.org/schema/beans"
    xmlns:http="http://www.mulesoft.org/schema/mule/http"
    xmlns:xsi="http://www.w3.org/2001/XMLSchema-instance"
    xmlns:context="http://www.springframework.org/schema/context"
    xmlns:geonames="http://www.mulesoft.org/schema/mule/geonames"
    xsi:schemaLocation="
        http://www.springframework.org/schema/beans
        http://www.springframework.org/schema/beans/spring-beans-3.0.xsd
        http://www.mulesoft.org/schema/mule/core
        http://www.mulesoft.org/schema/mule/core/current/mule.xsd
        http://www.mulesoft.org/schema/mule/http
        http://www.mulesoft.org/schema/mule/http/current/mule-http.xsd
        http://www.mulesoft.org/schema/mule/geonames
        http://www.mulesoft.org/schema/mule/geonames/current/mule-geonames.xsd">

        <spring:bean  id="objectStore"  class="org.mule.util.store.SimpleMemoryObject
Store" />

        <geonames:config username="demo" name="geonames" />

    <flow name="main">
        <http:inbound-endpoint host="localhost" port="8080"
            path="geonamesproxy" exchange-pattern="request-response" />

        <until-successful objectStore-ref="objectStore" maxRetries="5"
            secondsBetweenRetries="60">
            <geonames:find-nearby-pois-osm latitude="37.451" longitude="-122.18"
                config-ref="geonames" type="json" />
        </until-successful>
    </flow>

</mule>
```

Failure, by default, is defined as the encapsulated operation throwing an exception. It can also be configured to accept a `failureExpression` so that you can inspect the returned message and personally deem whether it is a failure or not:

```xml
<flow name="main">
  <http:inbound-endpoint host="localhost" port="8080"
    path="geonamesproxy" exchange-pattern="request-response" />

  <until-successful objectStore-ref="objectStore" maxRetries="5"
    secondsBetweenRetries="60" failureExpression="#[payload.contains('cafe')]">
    <geonames:find-nearby-pois-osm latitude="37.451" longitude="-122.18"
      config-ref="geonames" type="json" />
```

```
    </until-successful>
  </flow>
```

In this example, we define failure as the response body not containing the term "cafe." In more useful scenarios, you can check whether a resource has changed state, whether it has the correct amount of entries, and so on.

Once it has retried an operation the maximum amount of times, an exception is thrown by default. You can instead define a dead letter queue to handle the failing message:

```
<flow name="main">
  <http:inbound-endpoint host="localhost" port="8080"
   path="geonamesproxy" exchange-pattern="request-response" />

  <until-successful objectStore-ref="objectStore" maxRetries="5"
   secondsBetweenRetries="60" deadLetterQueue-ref="failed-messages">
  <geonames:find-nearby-pois-osm latitude="37.451" longitude="-122.18"
   config-ref="geonames" type="json" />
  </until-successful>
</flow>

<flow name="failed-messages">
  <logger level="ERROR" message="Message failed. Orignal message #[payload]" />
</flow>
```

In the previous example, we just route the failure to failed-messages flow where we simply log the message. You can instead configure this to write to a global endpoint (such as a JMS endpoint), if you desire.

> Be careful when using the until-successful router as it is asynchronous by default. Any subsequent message processors will not wait for the router to finish. However, In Mule version 3.5, this can be overridden by setting the synchronous attribute to true:
>
> ```
> <until-successful objectStore-ref="objectStore" maxRetries="5"
>  secondsBetweenRetries="60" deadLetterQueue-ref="failed-
> messages" synchronous="true">
> <geonames:find-nearby-pois-osm latitude="37.451"
> longitude="-122.18"
>  config-ref="geonames" type="json" />
> </until-successful>
> ```

Summary

In this chapter, we have introduced the building blocks to start creating real life integration applications. We now know how to configure and mashup multiple services while using different data formats and protocols.

The APIs we have used so far in this book are reasonably straightforward: read-only operations, no complex authorization mechanisms, etc. But even these types of APIs can be difficult to work with: the ones that make you jump through hoops in order to perform a task that should be dead simple to do.

The upcoming chapters will take a look at how we simplify even more complex APIs and deal with authorization, events, connection management, and more.

CHAPTER 4

OAuth Connectivity

On the Web, authentication is vital. Particularly with Open APIs, applications are relying more and more on resources that are spread all across the Web. Very few service providers offer APIs without some form of security or authorization. Some service providers just want to identify the consuming application via an API key, while others that deal with more sensitive user information have finer-grained authorization mechanisms such as *OAuth*.

To put OAuth into context, consider the following scenarios:

- An online photo lab printing your Flickr photos
- A social network using your Google address book to look for friends
- A fitness app that posts your progress to Twitter

It's great to utilize all these resources, but in order for these applications to access user data on other sites, they ask for usernames and passwords. Not only does this require exposing a user's password to some random application on the Web, but also provides these applications unlimited access to do as they wish.

So how do you allow a third-party application access to your account without disclosing your credentials? How can you grant partial access to your account, such as allowing an application to read your updates but not post any on your behalf? What if this third party application turns out to be malicious in some way? You need a way to revoke access at any time. These sort of situations are where OAuth comes in. OAuth provides a method for users to grant third-party access to their resources without sharing their passwords, and provides a way for users to grant and revoke specific access rights to their protected resources.

So how does OAuth enable this? Whatever you're using OAuth for, the end goal is always the same: you're trying to obtain an *access token* that your application can use to perform

API requests on behalf of a user. OAuth accomplishes this by requiring that the *consuming application* redirect the *user* or *resource owner* to the *service provider* to authenticate them with their *Authorization Server* and ultimately return the coveted access token to the consuming application. This access token can then be used on each request to the API to invoke operations on that user's behalf. This token can then be revoked by the user or service provider at any time without them sharing their username or password.

There are currently two main specifications for OAuth: OAuth v1.0a and OAuth v2, both very meaty. You'll want to visit here (*http://oauth.net/*) for a more detailed explanation, but Figure 4-1 illustrates the broad strokes of how a consuming application can authenticate a user with the service provider using the OAuth v2 specification.

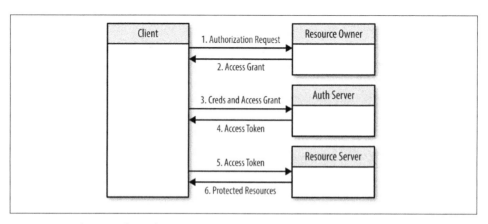

Figure 4-1. The OAuth v2 dance

As you can see, to access a protected API from within Mule would require a lot of development effort to handle all the requirements of the OAuth flow shown. However, Cloud Connectors abstract away all this complexity by providing a consistent approach for common OAuth tasks such as redirecting the user, callbacks, redirects customization, and managing consumer keys and access tokens. Throughout this chapter we will take a look at some popular APIs that use OAuth and show by example how Cloud Connectors simplify this process.

Configuring OAuth Connectors

Before you can start using an OAuth-protected API, you have to configure a few steps of the OAuth flow. The following sections will guide you through configuring these steps in detail.

Developer and Application Registration

OAuth requires that applications register with the authorization server so that API requests are able to be properly identified. Although the protocol allows for registration using automated means, most API providers require manual registration via filling out a form on their developer websites.

Once registered with the service provider, you will be provided with your application's authorization credentials, typically referred to as "consumer key" and "consumer secret" tokens. To demonstrate, we will first take a look at the LinkedIn connector as it uses OAuth as its authorization and authentication mechanism.

To add a new consuming application to LinkedIn, you will need to sign up for a developer account and follow the onscreen instructions. You'll want to visit here (*http://develop er.linkedin.com*) and read up on the full details, but Figure 4-2 demonstrates the broad strokes.

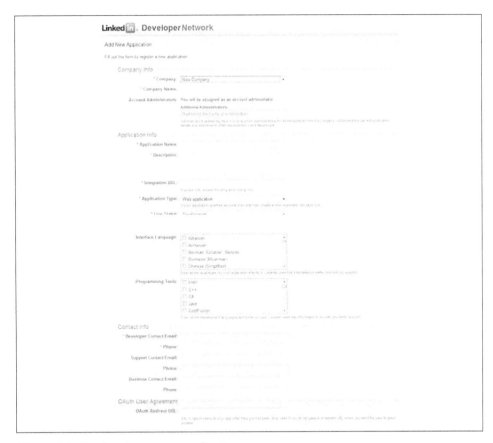

Figure 4-2. Configuring a new application

The process of obtaining these is explicitly outside the scope of the OAuth specification altogether, and is therefore defined by each service provider. This process needs to be completed only once per application, usually by the application developer herself, and is not considered one of the steps of the OAuth flow.

On this LinkedIn page, you can set up your new application, provide your application information, manage your OAuth settings, and obtain your API key. For this example, the important things here are setting the application type to "Web Application" to ensure that users are redirected back to the application after authorization and leaving the OAuth Redirect URL field empty. We intentionally leave this empty because we will pass this value to LinkedIn programmatically, which we will discuss shortly.

Configuring the Consumer Key and Consumer Secret

After you have the obtained credentials from the service provider as illustrated in the previous section, you can use these values to configure the connector. All connectors typically configure these at the `config` level, so they can be reused for all operations. But as mentioned previously, you can use multiple connector configurations if you need to use multiple accounts:

```xml
<?xml version="1.0" encoding="UTF-8"?>
<mule xmlns="http://www.mulesoft.org/schema/mule/core"
    xmlns:xsi="http://www.w3.org/2001/XMLSchema-instance"
    xmlns:linkedin="http://www.mulesoft.org/schema/mule/linkedin"
    xmlns:http="http://www.mulesoft.org/schema/mule/http"
    xsi:schemaLocation="
        http://www.mulesoft.org/schema/mule/core
        http://www.mulesoft.org/schema/mule/core/current/mule.xsd
        http://www.mulesoft.org/schema/mule/http
        http://www.mulesoft.org/schema/mule/http/current/mule-http.xsd
        http://www.mulesoft.org/schema/mule/linkedin
        http://www.mulesoft.org/schema/mule/linkedin/current/mule-linkedin.xsd">

    <linkedin:config name="linkedin" apiKey="${api.key}"
        apiSecret="${api.secret}">
        <linkedin:oauth-callback-config />
    <linkedin:config />

</mule>
```

Here we have set up the connector's `config` element with the two attributes: `apiKey` and `apiSecret`. These should be set to the values provided by the service provider. We are using mixed terminology for these tokens: sometimes "consumer key" and "consumer secret" and sometimes "api key" and "api secret." These terms are generally interchangeable and differ between the various connectors. Although it may seem confusing to use different terminology between different connectors, they can also reduce confusion by matching the semantics of the service provider's documentation.

Authorizing the Connector

In order to use an OAuth protected operation, we must first authorize the connector.

Redirecting for Authorization

All the operations within the LinkedIn connector are protected and need authorization. So before calling any connector operations, you must first authorize the connector by redirecting the user to the service provider to ultimately get the coveted access token that you can use for sending requests to the API. Of course, most of the gory details will be abstracted away, since you'll be using LinkedIn connector to do most of the tedious work. To accomplish this, all connectors created using the OAuth module provide a generic `authorize` operation that you can call to kick off the OAuth dance:

```xml
<?xml version="1.0" encoding="UTF-8"?>
<mule xmlns="http://www.mulesoft.org/schema/mule/core"
    xmlns:xsi="http://www.w3.org/2001/XMLSchema-instance"
    xmlns:linkedin="http://www.mulesoft.org/schema/mule/linkedin"
    xmlns:http="http://www.mulesoft.org/schema/mule/http"
    xsi:schemaLocation="
        http://www.mulesoft.org/schema/mule/core
        http://www.mulesoft.org/schema/mule/core/current/mule.xsd
        http://www.mulesoft.org/schema/mule/http
        http://www.mulesoft.org/schema/mule/http/current/mule-http.xsd
        http://www.mulesoft.org/schema/mule/linkedin
        http://www.mulesoft.org/schema/mule/linkedin/current/mule-linkedin.xsd">

    <linkedin:config name="linkedin" apiKey="${api.key}"
        apiSecret="${api.secret}">
        <linkedin:oauth-callback-config />
    <linkedin:config />

    <flow name="authorizationAndAuthenticationFlow">
        <http:inbound-endpoint host="localhost" port="8080"
            path="oauth-authorize" exchange-pattern="request-response" />

        <linkedin:authorize config-ref="linkedin" />
    </flow>
</mule>
```

As you can see, authorizing the connector is as simple as calling `linkedin:authorize`. Running this configuration will kick off the OAuth dance and redirect the user to LinkedIn for authorization (Figure 4-3). If an error occurs, or if a protected operation is invoked before calling `authorize`, the connector will throw a `NotAuthorizedExcep tion` and ask you to call the authorize connector properly.

It's important to note that the `inbound-endpoint` to this flow is `http`. The message source must always come from an HTTP inbound endpoint because the authorize process will reply with an HTTP redirect to the service provider, where the user can log in and authorize himself.

Figure 4-3. Browser redirect for authorization

So now that we have been redirected to LinkedIn for authorization, how do we get back to the Mule application? We mentioned earlier how we intentionally left the `Callback URL` field empty. It is this URL that is used to tell LinkedIn where to redirect the users back to after they have authorized themselves with the service provider.

When Mule redirects you to LinkedIn, it also generates an `inbound-endpoint` and a HTTP callback for you and passes the URL to the service provider programmatically. The connector will then listen for this callback. Once the user is authenticated, the service provider will call the callback URL to your application and the connector will switch to an authorized state.

LocalTunnel is a simple Ruby Gem that allows you to create a secure route through to your Internet-connected machine, providing a public URL that your development machine behind the firewall can use. With this URL, you can then customize your OAuth callback to work locally. Details on how to customize your OAuth callback URL can be found in "Customizing the Callback" on page 52.

Additional Authorization Parameters

Although Mule abstracts away the gory details of working with the Authorization Server and Access Token URLs, some additional, optional OAuth parameters can be sent across to the service provider that the connector simply cannot abstract away, because they require additional input from the end user.

state parameter

One particular case is the OAuth `state` parameter. For security purposes, the OAuth v2 specification allows an additional parameter to be sent across to the service provider during the redirect for authorization. This optional `state` parameter can be used by the client to maintain state between the request and callback.

The `authorize` operation of each connector, in turn, allows you to configure this parameter via the optional `state` attribute:

```
<linkedin:authorize state="#[UUID.randomUUID().toString()]"/>
```

This parameter should be a random unique string, unguessable and kept secret. When the service provider redirects the user back to your application, this parameter's value will be included in the response, so you can check it against the original value you sent in the request. The main purpose of this is to protect against cross-site request forgery (CSRF) (*http://en.wikipedia.org/wiki/Cross-site_request_forgery*). The previous example uses a simple embedded MEL expression to generate a pseudo-random UUID. After sending the state parameter to the service provider, it will be returned as an inbound message property that can simply be retrieved via MEL using:

```
<logger level="INFO" message="#[inboundProperties['state']]"/>
```

Custom parameters

The Authorization Server may also define additional parameters to be included and returned from calls to the Access Token URL or User Authorization URL. For example, the Salesforce Authorization server has a custom, optional `display` parameter outside of the OAuth specification. They use this parameter to tailor the login page's display type that the user will be redirected to based on the user's device: whether they are using a typical page display, a pop up, or a mobile device.

In these circumstances, additional parameters will be represented as optional attributes on the `authorize` operation itself:

```
<sfdc:authorize config-ref="salesforce-oauth" display="PAGE" />
```

This is a snippet of the Salesforce OAuth connector's `authorize` operation. If available or required, any additional parameters can be found at the connector's documentation page.

Accessing Protected Operations

Once the service provider hits the callback and the connector has switched to an authorized state, the OAuth state—such as access tokens—are stored in memory. This state information is later used by the connector on each call made to the service provider to let them know that we have already completed the authentication and authorization process. With this information, we can now call the connector's protected operations on that user's behalf:

```xml
<?xml version="1.0" encoding="UTF-8"?>
<mule xmlns="http://www.mulesoft.org/schema/mule/core"
    xmlns:xsi="http://www.w3.org/2001/XMLSchema-instance"
    xmlns:linkedin="http://www.mulesoft.org/schema/mule/linkedin"
    xmlns:http="http://www.mulesoft.org/schema/mule/http"
    xsi:schemaLocation="
        http://www.mulesoft.org/schema/mule/core
        http://www.mulesoft.org/schema/mule/core/current/mule.xsd
        http://www.mulesoft.org/schema/mule/http
        http://www.mulesoft.org/schema/mule/http/current/mule-http.xsd
        http://www.mulesoft.org/schema/mule/linkedin
        http://www.mulesoft.org/schema/mule/linkedin/current/mule-linkedin.xsd">

    <linkedin:config name="linkedin" apiKey="${api.key}"
        apiSecret="${api.secret}">
        <linkedin:oauth-callback-config />
    <linkedin:config />

    <flow name="authorizationAndAuthenticationFlow">
        <http:inbound-endpoint host="localhost" port="8080"
            path="oauth-authorize" exchange-pattern="request-response" />

        <linkedin:authorize config-ref="linkedin" />

        <linkedin:update-current-status
            status="Who says OAuth is difficult?!" />
    </flow>
</mule>
```

As you can see from the flow at the end of the previous example, defining a protected operation is the same as any other operation; there's no need to explicitly pass along access tokens. This is only a naive example that assumes a single-tenant application which will also redirect the user to the service provider each time it's invoked. A more practical example will be covered in "Saving and Restoring OAuth State" on page 55.

Customizing the Callback

As mentioned earlier, in order for the service provider to redirect users back to our application, we must provide them with a callback URL. OAuth-enabled connectors will automatically generate this for you and also provide additional settings to customize and generate your own.

Customizing the Callback URL

The URL generated for the callback URL is built using localhost as the host, the http.port environment variable or localPort variable as the port, and a randomly generated string as the path in the URL. If these settings are not suitable, you can override them in your connector configuration. Each connector that uses the generic OAuth module provides you with a oauth-callback-config element to override these settings.

Example 4-1 amends the previous example to add the additional oauth-callback-config configuration. The configuration takes three mandatory arguments: domain, localPort, and remotePort. These settings will be used to construct the callback URL that is passed to the external system. The URL will be the same as the default generated URL of the HTTP inbound endpoint, except that the host is replaced by the domain setting (or its default value) and the port is replaced by the remotePort setting (or its default value).

Example 4-1. Overriding default OAuth configuration

```xml
<?xml version="1.0" encoding="UTF-8"?>
<mule xmlns="http://www.mulesoft.org/schema/mule/core"
    xmlns:xsi="http://www.w3.org/2001/XMLSchema-instance"
    xmlns:linkedin="http://www.mulesoft.org/schema/mule/linkedin"
    xmlns:http="http://www.mulesoft.org/schema/mule/http"
    xsi:schemaLocation="
        http://www.mulesoft.org/schema/mule/core
        http://www.mulesoft.org/schema/mule/core/current/mule.xsd
        http://www.mulesoft.org/schema/mule/http
        http://www.mulesoft.org/schema/mule/http/current/mule-http.xsd
        http://www.mulesoft.org/schema/mule/linkedin
        http://www.mulesoft.org/schema/mule/linkedin/current/mule-linkedin.xsd">

    <http:connector name="http" />

    <linkedin:config name="linkedin" apiKey="${api.key}"
        apiSecret="${api.secret}">
        <linkedin:oauth-callback-config domain="localhost"
                    localPort="${http.port}" remotePort="${http.port}" connector-
ref="http" />
    </linkedin:config>

    <flow name="authorizationAndAuthenticationFlow">
        <http:inbound-endpoint host="localhost" port="8080"
            path="oauth-authorize" exchange-pattern="request-response" />

        <linkedin:authorize config-ref="linkedin" />
    </flow>
</mule>
```

Securing the Callback

Keep in mind that this callback URL is going to be wide open on the Internet, so steps should be taken to secure it. By default, some service providers will accept only HTTPS endpoints for security purposes in any case.

By default Mule will create only an HTTP endpoint. This can be overridden by passing in a reference to a predefined HTTPS connector through the optional `connector-ref` attribute.

Example 4-2 amends the previous OAuth example to use the HTTPS protocol for secure callbacks. This example defines first an additional HTTPS connector via the `https:con nector` element. This connector provides secure HTTP connectivity on top of what is already provided with the Mule HTTP transport. We have given the HTTPS connector a unique name via the `name` attribute to identify the connector. Lastly, the `http-callback-config` is exactly as done before, except that we have attached the additional `connector-ref` attribute that will indicate use of the HTTPS connector.

Example 4-2. Secure HTTPS OAuth implementation

```xml
<?xml version="1.0" encoding="UTF-8"?>
<mule xmlns="http://www.mulesoft.org/schema/mule/core"
    xmlns:xsi="http://www.w3.org/2001/XMLSchema-instance"
    xmlns:linkedin="http://www.mulesoft.org/schema/mule/linkedin"
    xmlns:http="http://www.mulesoft.org/schema/mule/http"
    xsi:schemaLocation="
        http://www.mulesoft.org/schema/mule/core
        http://www.mulesoft.org/schema/mule/core/current/mule.xsd
        http://www.mulesoft.org/schema/mule/http
        http://www.mulesoft.org/schema/mule/http/current/mule-http.xsd
        http://www.mulesoft.org/schema/mule/linkedin
        http://www.mulesoft.org/schema/mule/linkedin/current/mule-linkedin.xsd">

    <https:connector name="httpsConnector">
        <https:tls-key-store path="keystore.jks"
            keyPassword="mule2012" storePassword="mule2012" />
    </https:connector>

    <linkedin:config name="linkedin" apiKey="${api.key}" apiSecret="${api.secret}">
        <linkedin:oauth-callback-config
            domain="localhost"
            localPort="${http.port}"
            remotePort="${http.port}"
            connector-ref="httpsConnector" />
    </linkedin:config>

    <flow name="authorizationAndAuthenticationFlow">
        <http:inbound-endpoint host="localhost" port="8080"
            path="oauth-authorize" exchange-pattern="request-response" />

        <linkedin:authorize config-ref="linkedin" />
```

```
    </flow>
</mule>
```

More information on using the HTTPS connector and setting up trust stores can be found here (*http://bit.ly/mulesoft-documentation*).

Saving and Restoring OAuth State

After completing the initial OAuth dance, the access token and other OAuth state are kept in memory and reused by connector for subsequent calls to the API. You will probably need a way to persist this data so that it can be used in the future. For example, if the Mule instance goes down for any reason, the state is lost and the whole OAuth dance needs to be restarted. You also need a way to support multitenancy to be able to save multiple access tokens and to be able to restore them for the correct user.

To accomplish this, OAuth connectors can be divided into two subsets: connectors that use OAuth v2 and those that use OAuth v1.0a. The difference between them depends on whether or not the connector can automatically identify the user assigned to an access token. If it can, the connector will automatically save and restore the access token and will support multitenancy out of the box. If not, the connector will need some extra information from the end users of the connectors about how they want to store this information. Whichever subset you use, OAuth connectors provide consistent, easy-to-use hooks for saving and restoring this state information.

OAuth v2 State Management

As discussed, this form of state management is only supported by connectors that use OAuth v2. When using this subset of connector, the DevKit will automatically persist all the relevant information required to reuse an authorized connector. This information is currently as follows:

- The access token
- The access token secret (under OAuth 1.0a)
- The refresh token (under OAuth v2)
- Any information that was extracted during the service provider callback

Storing and retrieving access tokens

Authorizing the connector is the same as before, via the `authorize` operation. After invoking this operation, the information will be automatically stored in Mule's default user *object store*. An object store is an abstraction for storing objects in Mule. By using an object store, Mule is decoupled from any specific store implementation, allowing you to choose or switch the implementation at your discretion.

Once stored, the key to this information will be available to the user of the connector via a flow variable named OAuthAccessTokenId:

```xml
<?xml version="1.0" encoding="UTF-8"?>
<mule xmlns="http://www.mulesoft.org/schema/mule/core"
    xmlns:xsi="http://www.w3.org/2001/XMLSchema-instance"
    xmlns:spring="http://www.springframework.org/schema/beans"
    xmlns:context="http://www.springframework.org/schema/context"
    xmlns:sfdc="http://www.mulesoft.org/schema/mule/sfdc"
    xmlns:http="http://www.mulesoft.org/schema/mule/http"
    xsi:schemaLocation="
        http://www.mulesoft.org/schema/mule/core
        http://www.mulesoft.org/schema/mule/core/current/mule.xsd
        http://www.mulesoft.org/schema/mule/http
        http://www.mulesoft.org/schema/mule/http/current/mule-http.xsd
        http://www.mulesoft.org/schema/mule/sfdc
        http://www.mulesoft.org/schema/mule/sfdc/current/mule-sfdc.xsd
        http://www.springframework.org/schema/beans
        http://www.springframework.org/schema/beans/spring-beans-3.0.xsd
        http://www.springframework.org/schema/context
        http://www.springframework.org/schema/context/spring-context-3.0.xsd">

    <http:connector name="http" />

    <sfdc:config-with-oauth name="salesforce-oauth"
        consumerKey="yourConsumerKey" consumerSecret="yourConsumerSecret">
        <sfdc:oauth-callback-config domain="localhost" localPort="8081"
            remotePort="8081" path="oauthcallback" connector-ref="http" />
    </sfdc:config-with-oauth>

    <flow name="authorize">
        <http:inbound-endpoint host="localhost" port="8081"
            path="authorize" exchange-pattern="request-response" />

        <sfdc:authorize config-ref="salesforce-oauth" display="PAGE" />

        <logger level="INFO"
                message="The user identification is #[flowVars['OAuthAccessToke
nId']]" />
    </flow>

</mule>
```

This snippet uses the Salesforce OAuth connector for the purposes of demonstration. This flow authorizes the connector and simply logs the value of the OAuthAccess TokenId using the flowVars Mule expression.

As demonstrated, this information is only stored in a flow variable in the flowVars map by default. As indicated in "Variables and Expressions" on page 8, variables stored in flowVars are not propagated across Mule flows. So you may have to save the values in a different variable scope in order to use them within a different Mule flow. You can also expand the availability of a variable by saving the information instead in a cookie, a session variable, or any other place you see fit, so you can use it later within your flows.

The following is an example of storing the access token ID in a cookie and returning it to the client so that it can be sent back later to invoke protected operations:

```
<?xml version="1.0" encoding="UTF-8"?>
<mule xmlns="http://www.mulesoft.org/schema/mule/core"
    xmlns:xsi="http://www.w3.org/2001/XMLSchema-instance"
    xmlns:spring="http://www.springframework.org/schema/beans"
    xmlns:context="http://www.springframework.org/schema/context"
    xmlns:sfdc="http://www.mulesoft.org/schema/mule/sfdc"
    xmlns:http="http://www.mulesoft.org/schema/mule/http"
    xsi:schemaLocation="
        http://www.mulesoft.org/schema/mule/core
        http://www.mulesoft.org/schema/mule/core/current/mule.xsd
        http://www.mulesoft.org/schema/mule/http
        http://www.mulesoft.org/schema/mule/http/current/mule-http.xsd
        http://www.mulesoft.org/schema/mule/sfdc
        http://www.mulesoft.org/schema/mule/sfdc/current/mule-sfdc.xsd
        http://www.springframework.org/schema/beans
        http://www.springframework.org/schema/beans/spring-beans-3.0.xsd
        http://www.springframework.org/schema/context
        http://www.springframework.org/schema/context/spring-context-3.0.xsd">

    <http:connector name="http" />

    <sfdc:config-with-oauth name="salesforce-oauth"
        consumerKey="yourConsumerKey" consumerSecret="yourConsumerSecret">
        <sfdc:oauth-callback-config domain="localhost" localPort="8081"
            remotePort="8081" path="oauthcallback" connector-ref="http" />
    </sfdc:config-with-oauth>

    <flow name="authorize">
        <http:inbound-endpoint host="localhost" port="8081"
            path="authorize" exchange-pattern="request-response" />

        <sfdc:authorize config-ref="salesforce-oauth" display="PAGE" />

        <logger level="INFO"
            message="The user identification is #[flowVars[
                    'OAuthAccessTokenId']]" />

        <http:response-builder status="200">
            <http:set-cookie name="accessTokenId"
                value="#[flowVars['OAuthAccessTokenId']]"/>
            <set-payload
                    value="You access token id is #[flowVars['OAuthAccessToke
nId']]"/>
        </http:response-builder>
    </flow>
```

```
    </mule>
```

Once you have retrieved the identifier, you can then use it to invoke API operations. Each operation that is protected by OAuth will provide an optional attribute called accessTokenId. This access token ID is the ID of the access token you stored, and will be used to make the call.

Keep in mind that the accessTokenId is *not* the access token itself, and represents more than the access token: it points to all the information in the stored OAuth state.

The following example amends the earlier flow to use the accessTokenId as an argument to the sfdc:get-user-info operation. Once invoked, two things can happen. First, Mule will try to retrieve the connector that is already loaded in memory. If it is not found, Mule will look in the object store and retrieve the previously obtained access token for that user:

```
<?xml version="1.0" encoding="UTF-8"?>
<mule xmlns="http://www.mulesoft.org/schema/mule/core"
    xmlns:xsi="http://www.w3.org/2001/XMLSchema-instance"
    xmlns:spring="http://www.springframework.org/schema/beans"
    xmlns:context="http://www.springframework.org/schema/context"
    xmlns:sfdc="http://www.mulesoft.org/schema/mule/sfdc"
    xmlns:http="http://www.mulesoft.org/schema/mule/http"
    xsi:schemaLocation="
        http://www.mulesoft.org/schema/mule/core
        http://www.mulesoft.org/schema/mule/core/current/mule.xsd
        http://www.mulesoft.org/schema/mule/http
        http://www.mulesoft.org/schema/mule/http/current/mule-http.xsd
        http://www.mulesoft.org/schema/mule/sfdc
        http://www.mulesoft.org/schema/mule/sfdc/current/mule-sfdc.xsd
        http://www.springframework.org/schema/beans
        http://www.springframework.org/schema/beans/spring-beans-3.0.xsd
        http://www.springframework.org/schema/context
        http://www.springframework.org/schema/context/spring-context-3.0.xsd">

    <http:connector name="http" enableCookies="true" />

    <sfdc:config-with-oauth name="salesforce-oauth"
        consumerKey="yourConsumerKey" consumerSecret="yourConsumerSecret">
        <sfdc:oauth-callback-config domain="localhost" localPort="8081"
            remotePort="8081" path="oauthcallback" connector-ref="http" />
    </sfdc:config-with-oauth>

    <flow name="authorize">
        <http:inbound-endpoint host="localhost" port="8081"
            path="authorize" exchange-pattern="request-response" />
```

```
            <sfdc:authorize config-ref="salesforce-oauth" display="PAGE" />

            <http:response-builder status="200">
                <http:set-cookie name="accessTokenId"
                    value="#[flowVars['OAuthAccessTokenId']]"/>
                <set-payload
                        value="Your access token id is #[flowVars['OAuthAccessToke
nId']]"/>
            </http:response-builder>
        </flow>

    <flow name="getUser">
        <http:inbound-endpoint host="localhost" port="8081"
            path="getUser" exchange-pattern="request-response" />

        <sfdc:get-user-info config-ref="salesforce-oauth"
            accessTokenId="#[($ in Arrays.asList(message.inboundProperties['coo
kies']) if $.name == 'accessTokenId')[0].value]" />
    </flow>
<mule>
```

Using the previous example, the first flow "authorize" will return a cookie named ac
cessTokenId, which is then required to invoke the second flow "getUser." Here we are
using a MEL expression to extract the cookie from the incoming request to invoke the
protected operation.

Multitenant access tokens

Each OAuth-enabled connector is perfectly capable of being multitenant. This basically
means that the same application and the same instance of the connector can serve multiple users at the same time. As we saw in the previous examples, Mule stores all OAuth
user information within an object store so it can be retrieved later to invoke protected
operations. Since an object store is comprised of key/value pairs, each user entry must
be given an ID to identify a particular user. This ID is the OAuthAccessTokenID variable
that we used in the previous example. Prior to Mule 3.5, this ID is automatically generated by the connector using something unique from the service provider such as your
Salesforce username for example. However, how does your application know which
access ID to retrieve? Well, in short—it doesn't. If your application is multitenant, you
need a way to map one of your applications users (say, *ryan@yourawesomeapp.com*) to
an access token ID (say, *ryan@salesforce.com*).

Since Mule 3.5, all access tokens are stored under a default key that matches the connector's config name. So in the previous example, the Salesforce connector instance
we're using has the name "salesforce-oauth," and in turn the OAuthAccessTokenID will
be "salesforce-oauth." As you can probably tell, this doesn't work in a multitenant environment as each new user would override the previous and users would be forced to
reauthorize themselves each time. Fortunately, Mule 3.5+ provides a simple hook to

allow you to store and retrieve an access token using a user-defined expression. This enables you to provide your own ID for a unique user so your application can become truly multitenant. Let's have a look at how we can modify the previous example to support multitenancy:

```xml
<?xml version="1.0" encoding="UTF-8"?>
<mule xmlns="http://www.mulesoft.org/schema/mule/core"
    xmlns:xsi="http://www.w3.org/2001/XMLSchema-instance"
    xmlns:spring="http://www.springframework.org/schema/beans"
    xmlns:context="http://www.springframework.org/schema/context"
    xmlns:sfdc="http://www.mulesoft.org/schema/mule/sfdc"
    xmlns:http="http://www.mulesoft.org/schema/mule/http"
    xsi:schemaLocation="
        http://www.mulesoft.org/schema/mule/core
        http://www.mulesoft.org/schema/mule/core/current/mule.xsd
        http://www.mulesoft.org/schema/mule/http
        http://www.mulesoft.org/schema/mule/http/current/mule-http.xsd
        http://www.mulesoft.org/schema/mule/sfdc
        http://www.mulesoft.org/schema/mule/sfdc/current/mule-sfdc.xsd
        http://www.springframework.org/schema/beans
        http://www.springframework.org/schema/beans/spring-beans-3.0.xsd
        http://www.springframework.org/schema/context
        http://www.springframework.org/schema/context/spring-context-3.0.xsd">

    <http:connector name="http" />

    <sfdc:config-with-oauth name="salesforce-oauth"
        consumerKey="yourConsumerKey" consumerSecret="yourConsumerSecret">
        <sfdc:oauth-callback-config domain="localhost" localPort="8081"
            remotePort="8081" path="oauthcallback" connector-ref="http" />
    </sfdc:config-with-oauth>

    <flow name="authorize">
        <http:inbound-endpoint host="localhost" port="8081"
            path="authorize" exchange-pattern="request-response"/>

        <sfdc:authorize config-ref="salesforce-oauth" display="PAGE"
            accessTokenId="#[inboundProperties['tenantId']]" />

    </flow>

    <flow name="getUser">
        <http:inbound-endpoint host="localhost" port="8081"
            path="getUser" exchange-pattern="request-response" />

        <sfdc:get-user-info config-ref="salesforce-oauth"
            accessTokenId="#[inboundProperties['tenantId']]" />
    </flow>
<mule>
```

The previous example amended the authorize operation with an additional attribute named accessTokenId. This attribute allows you specify a custom ID of your choice to store the access token in the object store. This is an optional parameter; if unspecified, it will take the config's name by default. But if you do specify it, the token key will be forced to the value provided. This ID can then be passed to the protected operation directly in subsequent flows.

 The accessTokenId attribute and the defaulting of the ID to the config's name is a new feature in Mule 3.5. To emulate this functionality in previous versions, you need to use an enricher and the object store module to manually store and retrieve these IDs yourself.

Overriding the default object store

The connector will use the default user object store to save the OAuth state. In most cases, this object store will meet your needs and no extra configuration is necessary. However, you can override this behavior and specify an object store of choice via the config-level element oauth-store-config:

```xml
<?xml version="1.0" encoding="UTF-8"?>
<mule xmlns="http://www.mulesoft.org/schema/mule/core"
    xmlns:xsi="http://www.w3.org/2001/XMLSchema-instance"
    xmlns:spring="http://www.springframework.org/schema/beans"
    xmlns:context="http://www.springframework.org/schema/context"
    xmlns:sfdc="http://www.mulesoft.org/schema/mule/sfdc"
    xmlns:http="http://www.mulesoft.org/schema/mule/http"
    xsi:schemaLocation="
        http://www.mulesoft.org/schema/mule/core
        http://www.mulesoft.org/schema/mule/core/current/mule.xsd
        http://www.mulesoft.org/schema/mule/http
        http://www.mulesoft.org/schema/mule/http/current/mule-http.xsd
        http://www.mulesoft.org/schema/mule/sfdc
        http://www.mulesoft.org/schema/mule/sfdc/current/mule-sfdc.xsd
        http://www.springframework.org/schema/beans
        http://www.springframework.org/schema/beans/spring-beans-3.0.xsd
        http://www.springframework.org/schema/context
        http://www.springframework.org/schema/context/spring-context-3.0.xsd">

    <http:connector name="http" />

    <sfdc:config-with-oauth name="salesforce-oauth"
        consumerKey="yourConsumerKey" consumerSecret="yourConsumerSecret">
        <sfdc:oauth-callback-config domain="localhost" localPort="8081"
            remotePort="8081" path="oauthcallback" connector-ref="http" />
        <sfdc:oauth-store-config
            objectStore-ref="_defaultInMemoryObjectStore" />
    </sfdc:config-with-oauth>

    <flow name="authorize">
        <http:inbound-endpoint host="localhost" port="8081"
            path="authorize" exchange-pattern="request-response" />
```

```
        <sfdc:authorize config-ref="salesforce-oauth" display="PAGE" />

        <sfdc:get-user-info config-ref="salesforce-oauth"
            accessTokenId="#[flowVars['OAuthAccessTokenId']]" />
    </flow>
</mule>
```

Here, the example from the previous section has been amended to include the new
oauth-store-config element. This element contains a single attribute that passes in an
object store by reference. Here we are just passing a reference to the default object store,
but you can use a persistent object store or a custom one of your own. More on available
and custom object stores can be found at its documentation page (*http://bit.ly/
1nfCRYO*).

OAuth v1.0a State Management

The automatic OAuth state management features are only available for OAuth v2 connectors. Prior to this, the saving and restoring of this state needed to be done manually.
Some connectors are still using the manual state management technique and others still
need to do so when users cannot be easily identified and associated with an access token.
Although I am referring to this process as "manual," this subset of OAuth connectors
still provides useful hooks to make this functionality easy to use.

To enable this functionality, connectors that require manual state management provide
a set of message processors for serializing the state yourself, via save-oauth-access-
token and restore-oauth-access-token elements. Both elements work off a set of
properties on the Mule message named OAuthAccessToken and OAuthAccessToken
Secret.

When using this functionality, on the initial call to authorize, the connector will first
invoke the restore-oauth-access-token message processor to check that a message
property named OAuthAccessToken exists on the Mule message. As it is the first call,
no property will exist, so it will initiate the OAuth dance as usual. Once the initial OAuth
dance is complete, the connector will invoke save-oauth-access-token message and
add two new inbound properties on the Mule message named OAuthAccessToken and
OAuthAccessTokenSecret. As no one size fits all, it is up to you, the developer, to decide
where you want to save these properties. You can save them to a database using the
JDBC transport or a file using the File transport; whatever is appropriate for your environment. To demonstrate, we will use the Mule ObjectStore Module to persist the
properties:

```
<?xml version="1.0" encoding="UTF-8"?>
<mule xmlns="http://www.mulesoft.org/schema/mule/core"
    xmlns:xsi="http://www.w3.org/2001/XMLSchema-instance"
    xmlns:linkedin="http://www.mulesoft.org/schema/mule/linkedin"
    xmlns:objectstore="http://www.mulesoft.org/schema/mule/objectstore"
```

```
    xmlns:http="http://www.mulesoft.org/schema/mule/http"
    xsi:schemaLocation="
        http://www.mulesoft.org/schema/mule/core
        http://www.mulesoft.org/schema/mule/core/current/mule.xsd
        http://www.mulesoft.org/schema/mule/http
        http://www.mulesoft.org/schema/mule/http/current/mule-http.xsd
        http://www.mulesoft.org/schema/mule/objectstore
                    http://www.mulesoft.org/schema/mule/objectstore/current/mule-
objectstore.xsd
        http://www.mulesoft.org/schema/mule/linkedin
        http://www.mulesoft.org/schema/mule/linkedin/current/mule-linkedin.xsd">

    <http:connector name="http" />

        <linkedin:config name="linkedin" apiKey="${api.key}" apiSecret="${api.se
cret}">
        <linkedin:oauth-callback-config
            domain="localhost" localPort="${http.port}"
            remotePort="${http.port}" connector-ref="http" />
        <linkedin:oauth-save-access-token>
            <objectstore:store
                key="OAuthAccessToken"
                value-ref="#[inboundProperties['OAuthAccessToken']]"/>
            <objectstore:store
                key="OAuthAccessTokenSecret"
                value-ref="#[inboundProperties[
                        'OAuthAccessTokenSecret']]"/>
        </linkedin:oauth-save-access-token>
    </linkedin:config>

    <flow name="authorizationAndAuthenticationFlow">
        <http:inbound-endpoint host="localhost" port="8080"
            path="oauth-authorize" exchange-pattern="request-response" />

        <linkedin:authorize config-ref="linkedin" />
    </flow>
</mule>
```

This example simply accesses the new parameters from the message using the MEL
expression's `#[inboundProperties['OAuthAccessToken']]` and `inboundProperties`
`['OAuthAccessTokenSecret']]` and then adding them to our object store.

With the access tokens saved, we need a way of restoring them. When the initial OAuth
dance starts, Mule will first invoke the `restore-oauth-access-token` message processor. Just like `save-oauth-access-token`, this message processor is responsible for
using the `OAuthAccessToken` and `OAuthAccessTokenSecret` properties, but this time
in reverse. This time it is responsible for creating these properties on the message and
adding them to the outbound scope:

```
<?xml version="1.0" encoding="UTF-8"?>
<mule xmlns="http://www.mulesoft.org/schema/mule/core"
```

```
        xmlns:xsi="http://www.w3.org/2001/XMLSchema-instance"
        xmlns:linkedin="http://www.mulesoft.org/schema/mule/linkedin"
        xmlns:objectstore="http://www.mulesoft.org/schema/mule/objectstore"
        xmlns:http="http://www.mulesoft.org/schema/mule/http"
        xsi:schemaLocation="
            http://www.mulesoft.org/schema/mule/core
            http://www.mulesoft.org/schema/mule/core/current/mule.xsd
            http://www.mulesoft.org/schema/mule/http
            http://www.mulesoft.org/schema/mule/http/current/mule-http.xsd
            http://www.mulesoft.org/schema/mule/objectstore
                        http://www.mulesoft.org/schema/mule/objectstore/current/mule-
    objectstore.xsd
            http://www.mulesoft.org/schema/mule/linkedin
            http://www.mulesoft.org/schema/mule/linkedin/current/mule-linkedin.xsd">

        <http:connector name="http" />

            <linkedin:config name="linkedin" apiKey="${api.key}" apiSecret="${api.se
    cret}">
            <linkedin:oauth-callback-config
                domain="localhost" localPort="${http.port}"
                remotePort="${http.port}" connector-ref="http" />
            <linkedin:oauth-save-access-token>
                <objectstore:store
                    key="OAuthAccessToken"
                    value-ref="#[inboundProperties['OAuthAccessToken']]"/>
                <objectstore:store
                    key="OAuthAccessTokenSecret"
                    value-ref="#[inboundProperties['OAuthAccessTokenSecret']]"/>
            </linkedin:oauth-save-access-token>
            <linkedin:oauth-restore-access-token>
                <enricher target="#[outboundProperties['OAuthAccessToken']]">
                    <objectstore:retrieve
                        key="OAuthAccessToken"/>
                </enricher>
                <enricher target="#[outboundProperties['OAuthAccessTokenSecret']]">
                    <objectstore:retrieve
                        key="OAuthAccessTokenSecret"/>
                </enricher>
            </linkedin:oauth-restore-access-token>
        <linkedin:config>

        <flow name="authorizationAndAuthenticationFlow">
            <http:inbound-endpoint host="localhost" port="8080"
                path="oauth-authorize exchange-pattern="request-response" />

            <linkedin:authorize config-ref="linkedin" />
        </flow>
    </mule>
```

In this example, we are using the enricher element to set the required properties. This particular flow uses an enricher to add a property to the current message with the value

that the `objectstore:retrieve` endpoint returns. In this case, `#[outboundProper`
`ties['OAuthAccessTokenSecret']]`, which adds/overwrites the specified message
header `OAuthAccessTokenSecret` within the outbound property scope.

Unauthorizing the Connector

Just as you call the `authorize` operation to authorize the connector with the service
provider, connectors provide another operation to unauthorize the connector, via the
aptly named `unauthorize` element:

```xml
<?xml version="1.0" encoding="UTF-8"?>
<mule xmlns="http://www.mulesoft.org/schema/mule/core"
    xmlns:xsi="http://www.w3.org/2001/XMLSchema-instance"
    xmlns:linkedin="http://www.mulesoft.org/schema/mule/linkedin"
    xmlns:objectstore="http://www.mulesoft.org/schema/mule/objectstore"
    xmlns:http="http://www.mulesoft.org/schema/mule/http"
    xsi:schemaLocation="
        http://www.mulesoft.org/schema/mule/core
        http://www.mulesoft.org/schema/mule/core/current/mule.xsd
        http://www.mulesoft.org/schema/mule/http
        http://www.mulesoft.org/schema/mule/http/current/mule-http.xsd
        http://www.mulesoft.org/schema/mule/objectstore
                    http://www.mulesoft.org/schema/mule/objectstore/current/mule-
objectstore.xsd
        http://www.mulesoft.org/schema/mule/linkedin
        http://www.mulesoft.org/schema/mule/linkedin/current/mule-linkedin.xsd">

    <http:connector name="http" />

        <linkedin:config  name="linkedin"  apiKey="${api.key}"  apiSecret="${api.se
cret}">
        <linkedin:oauth-callback-config
            domain="localhost" localPort="${http.port}"
            remotePort="${http.port}" connector-ref="http" />
        <linkedin:oauth-save-access-token>
            <objectstore:store
                key="OAuthAccessToken"
                value-ref="#[inboundProperties['OAuthAccessToken']]"/>
            <objectstore:store key="OAuthAccessTokenSecret"
                value-ref="#[inboundProperties['OAuthAccessTokenSecret']]"/>
        </linkedin:oauth-save-access-token>
        <linkedin:oauth-restore-access-token>
            <enricher target="#[outboundProperties['OAuthAccessToken']]">
                <objectstore:retrieve key="OAuthAccessToken"/>
            </enricher>
            <enricher target="#[outboundProperties['OAuthAccessTokenSecret']]">
                <objectstore:retrieve key="OAuthAccessTokenSecret"/>
            </enricher>
        </linkedin:oauth-restore-access-token>
    <linkedin:config>
```

```
<flow name="authorizationAndAuthenticationFlow">
    <http:inbound-endpoint  host="localhost" port="8080"
        path="oauth-authorize exchange-pattern="request-response" />

    <linkedin:authorize config-ref="linkedin" />

    <linkedin:update-current-status config-ref="linkedin"
        status="Who says OAuth is difficult?!" />

    <linkedin:unauthorize config-ref="linkedin" />
</flow>
</mule>
```

This example authorizes the connector and calls the API, as in previous examples. Additionally, we then unauthorize the connector using the `unauthorize` operation. After this operation is called, the stored access tokens will be cleaned out from the object store and the connector will need reauthorization in order to be used again. Whereas previous examples redirect you only on the first call to `authorize`, this flow will force you to be redirected each time.

Two-Legged OAuth and Other Variations

The OAuth process we have been using throughout these examples is also referred to as three-legged OAuth, with the three legs being the interactions between the three parties involved: your consuming application, the service provider, and the user. The OAuth 1.0 and 2 specifications all outline this three-legged process, but there are also other variations such as two-legged OAuth and some service providers' own custom interpretations of OAuth.

There is great debate and no official specification on what constitutes as two-legged OAuth. However, for the purposes of this book, two-legged Oauth can be defined as skipping user authorization altogether, whereby the user does not need to be redirected for authorization because he is not requesting access to any user data.

Another good example of these variations is Twitter. Twitter has an option that is different from this again where it provides access to a user's preexisting data via a manually obtained access token. This is different from two-legged OAuth because we are using a specific user's data, but is similar in that it allows consumers to skip the OAuth dance completely and send the access tokens through directly, analogous to a username/password system.

Developer and Application Registration

After you have created an application through Twitter (*https://dev.twitter.com/*), you will be given the option to generate your own access tokens for your specific user account

---

(Figure 4-4). Once that's complete, Twitter will provide you with your access token and access token secret.

Figure 4-4. Twitter application registration: generate your own access tokens

Configuring the Access Tokens

Manually obtained access tokens can then be configured at the connector's config level. Each subsequent connector operation will execute on behalf of the user account referenced by the hardcoded access token and access token secret, without redirecting for authorization:

```xml
<?xml version="1.0" encoding="UTF-8"?>
<mule xmlns="http://www.mulesoft.org/schema/mule/core"
    xmlns:xsi="http://www.w3.org/2001/XMLSchema-instance"
    xmlns:spring="http://www.springframework.org/schema/beans"
    xmlns:context="http://www.springframework.org/schema/context"
    xmlns:twitter="http://www.mulesoft.org/schema/mule/twitter"
    xmlns:http="http://www.mulesoft.org/schema/mule/http"
    xsi:schemaLocation="
        http://www.mulesoft.org/schema/mule/core
        http://www.mulesoft.org/schema/mule/core/current/mule.xsd
        http://www.mulesoft.org/schema/mule/http
        http://www.mulesoft.org/schema/mule/http/current/mule-http.xsd
        http://www.mulesoft.org/schema/mule/twitter
        http://www.mulesoft.org/schema/mule/twitter/current/mule-twitter.xsd
        http://www.springframework.org/schema/beans
        http://www.springframework.org/schema/beans/spring-beans-3.0.xsd
        http://www.springframework.org/schema/context
        http://www.springframework.org/schema/context/spring-context-3.0.xsd">

    <twitter:config name="twitter" consumerKey="${twitter.consumer.key}"
            consumerSecret="${twitter.consumer.secret}" accessKey="${twitter.ac
cess.key}"
            accessSecret="${twitter.access.secret}" />

    <flow name="twitterFlow1">
```

```
        <http:inbound-endpoint host="localhost" port="8081"
            path="addtweet" exchange-pattern="request-response" />

        <twitter:update-status config-ref="twitter"
            status="tweet tweet" />
    </flow>
</mule>
```

Authorizing the Connector

If instead you want the Twitter connector to redirect the user for authorization, you can remove the hardcoded access key and secret and request authorization in a similar fashion to the LinkedIn example, as follows:

```
<?xml version="1.0" encoding="UTF-8"?>
<mule xmlns="http://www.mulesoft.org/schema/mule/core"
    xmlns:xsi="http://www.w3.org/2001/XMLSchema-instance"
    xmlns:spring="http://www.springframework.org/schema/beans"
    xmlns:context="http://www.springframework.org/schema/context"
    xmlns:twitter="http://www.mulesoft.org/schema/mule/twitter"
    xmlns:http="http://www.mulesoft.org/schema/mule/http"
    xsi:schemaLocation="
        http://www.mulesoft.org/schema/mule/core
        http://www.mulesoft.org/schema/mule/core/current/mule.xsd
        http://www.mulesoft.org/schema/mule/http
        http://www.mulesoft.org/schema/mule/http/current/mule-http.xsd
        http://www.mulesoft.org/schema/mule/twitter
        http://www.mulesoft.org/schema/mule/twitter/current/mule-twitter.xsd
        http://www.springframework.org/schema/beans
        http://www.springframework.org/schema/beans/spring-beans-3.0.xsd
        http://www.springframework.org/schema/context
        http://www.springframework.org/schema/context/spring-context-3.0.xsd">

    <twitter:config name="twitter" consumerKey="${twitter.consumer.key}"
        consumerSecret="${twitter.consumer.secret}" />

    <flow name="twitterFlow1">
        <http:inbound-endpoint host="localhost" port="8081"
            path="addtweet" exchange-pattern="request-response" />

        <twitter:request-authorization config-ref="twitter" />

        <twitter:update-status config-ref="twitter"
            status="tweet tweet" />
    </flow>
</mule>
```

Note that this does not follow the normal OAuth message processors by using the `authorize` message processor, but instead uses the `request-authorization` message processor. This is because the Twitter connector was created before the OAuth modules were introduced. Instead, the connector uses the Twitter4j libraries under the covers to handle OAuth. This means that certain OAuth functionality provided by the generic OAuth module is not available for this connector.

Summary

At first glance, the task of implementing OAuth can appear daunting, and OAuth's token exchange system can be confusing if you're unfamiliar with it. Fortunately, Cloud Connectors have done the groundwork for us and OAuth clients are now just a few lines of XML.

We have barely touched the full OAuth specifications or discussed things like refresh tokens. That's the beauty of it: we don't need to.

CHAPTER 5

Connection Management

As we have seen so far, Cloud Connectors abstract away most of the fuss of dealing with APIs: we haven't needed to know whether a service provider is a REST-based service, a SOAP-based service, or some other custom protocol on top of TCP. But when service providers have more stateful protocols that require the management and sharing of connections, they may need some additional input from the end user of the connector to manage its state.

To put connection management into context, many early APIs, and some current APIs as well, support session-based authentication. In these schemes, the user typically first has to call a "login" method, which takes a username/password combination as input and returns a unique session key that represents that user's session. The user must then include this session key in each request to the API, and then call "logout" when he is finished. Figure 5-1 illustrates a typical session-based authentication scheme.

This type of authentication maps very naturally to a website because users are accustomed to "logging in" when they start working with a particular site and "logging out" when they are done. But when it comes to web APIs, this proves more difficult because the client must keep track of state, manage concurrent sessions, worry about session timeouts, etc.

Instead, Cloud Connectors abstract away these types of processes and offer automatic connection management that will handle connecting, disconnecting, validating connections, getting a session identifier, and so on. This chapter will discuss in detail how to configure connection management features and fine tune your connectors for both performance and reliability.

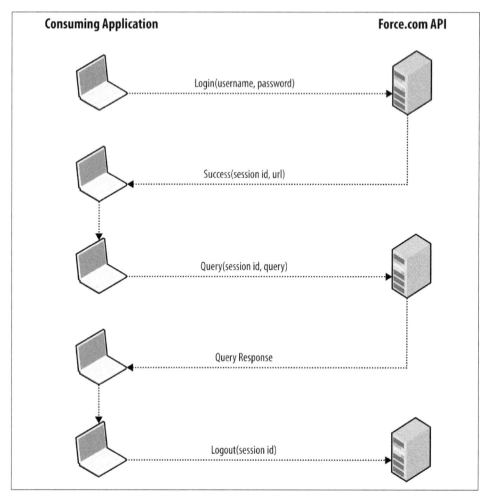

Figure 5-1. Session-based authentication

Configuring Connection Management

Connection management enabled connectors provide specific settings and configuration to enable both multitenancy and the management and sharing of connections.

Pooling Connections

Connection pooling is an important concept in most development environments because the performance cost of establishing a connection to another data source, such as a database, is relatively high. This is no different when using web APIs; creating one or more new connections for every request creates an unnecessary burden and leads to weaker performance.

Take Salesforce, for example. Salesforce offers a full range of APIs, including SOAP, REST, BULK, METADATA, and APEX. The SOAP API authenticates API calls using a typical session-based authentication scheme via a login( ) operation and a logout( ) operation, and returns a unique session for each user account. Calling these login and logout methods every time you work with the API wastes resources. Instead, you should maintain a pool of connections and reuse these sessions when possible. However, this brings its own challenges: maintaining a connection pool, validating connections, removing expired connections, etc.

Cloud Connectors do exactly this and abstract away the complexity of maintaining your own pool of connectors. Example 5-1 demonstrates the use of the Salesforce Cloud Connector with the Salesforce SOAP API.

Example 5-1. Salesforce session example

```xml
<?xml version="1.0" encoding="UTF-8"?>
<mule xmlns="http://www.mulesoft.org/schema/mule/core"
    xmlns:sfdc="http://www.mulesoft.org/schema/mule/sfdc"
    xmlns:http="http://www.mulesoft.org/schema/mule/http"
    xmlns:spring="http://www.springframework.org/schema/beans"
    xmlns:core="http://www.mulesoft.org/schema/mule/core"
    xmlns:xsi="http://www.w3.org/2001/XMLSchema-instance"
    xsi:schemaLocation="
        http://www.mulesoft.org/schema/mule/sfdc
        http://www.mulesoft.org/schema/mule/sfdc/current/mule-sfdc.xsd
        http://www.mulesoft.org/schema/mule/http
        http://www.mulesoft.org/schema/mule/http/current/mule-http.xsd
        http://www.springframework.org/schema/beans
        http://www.springframework.org/schema/beans/spring-beans-current.xsd
        http://www.mulesoft.org/schema/mule/core
        http://www.mulesoft.org/schema/mule/core/current/mule.xsd">

    <sfdc:config name="salesforce"
        username="${salesforce.username}" password="${salesforce.password}"
        securityToken="${salesforce.securityToken}" />

    <flow name="salesforceSession">
        <http:inbound-endpoint host="localhost" port="8081"
            path="salesforce" />

        <sfdc:get-user-info config-ref="salesforce" />
    </flow>
</mule>
```

This configuration uses the get-user-info operation that queries the Salesforce SOAP API to simply return the information for the current user. As you can see from the flow at the end of the example, there is no need to specifically call a "login" operation to start using the API or a "logout" operation when finished. Instead, we simply use a connector operation to query the API as usual.

This configuration will automatically manage the Salesforce session for the specified user, logging in and out and reusing the session ID on future invocations, thus saving both time and resources when connecting to the API each time.

Connection Parameters and Multitenancy

In order to pool connections, connectors require certain connection parameters to be declared for establishing connections and borrowing and returning connections within the pool. The Salesforce connector uses the following three parameters: username, password, and securityToken. These parameters are required by the connection management features to establish each and every connection. Behind the scenes, it will also use one of these parameters as the key to the connection pool—in this case, the username parameter. When you execute a connector operation, the connector will attempt to look up an already established connection using this key. If none exists, the connector will create one. Once complete, it will return it to the connection pool.

As we have set the connection parameters at the config level, they will be used for all operations and you will always have at most one user session. To support multiple user sessions, each connector that supports connection management also allows you to specify connection parameters as arguments to individual connector operations and will override whatever is specified at the config level. When used at the operation level (i.e., not in config), the connectors allow you to pool multiple sessions and benefit from full expression evaluation so you can do things like extract connection details from an incoming Mule message and thus create new connections with the API at runtime. Example 5-2 amends the previous example, configuring the connection parameters at the operation level opposed to the config level.

Example 5-2. Operation level connection parameters

```xml
<?xml version="1.0" encoding="UTF-8"?>
<mule xmlns="http://www.mulesoft.org/schema/mule/core"
    xmlns:sfdc="http://www.mulesoft.org/schema/mule/sfdc"
    xmlns:http="http://www.mulesoft.org/schema/mule/http"
    xmlns:spring="http://www.springframework.org/schema/beans"
    xmlns:core="http://www.mulesoft.org/schema/mule/core"
    xmlns:xsi="http://www.w3.org/2001/XMLSchema-instance"
    xsi:schemaLocation="
        http://www.mulesoft.org/schema/mule/sfdc
        http://www.mulesoft.org/schema/mule/sfdc/current/mule-sfdc.xsd
        http://www.mulesoft.org/schema/mule/http
        http://www.mulesoft.org/schema/mule/http/current/mule-http.xsd
        http://www.springframework.org/schema/beans
        http://www.springframework.org/schema/beans/spring-beans-current.xsd
        http://www.mulesoft.org/schema/mule/core
        http://www.mulesoft.org/schema/mule/core/current/mule.xsd">

    <sfdc:config name="salesforce" />
```

```
    <flow name="salesforceSession">
        <http:inbound-endpoint host="localhost" port="8081"
            path="salesforce" />

        <sfdc:get-user-info username="${salesforce.username}"
            password="${salesforce.password}" securityToken="${salesforce.securityTo
ken}"
            config-ref="salesforce" />
    </flow>
</mule>
```

If you run this operation twice in quick succession, you will see that the same session
ID is logged and that the connector instance is reused. If you allow time for the connection to become idle and rerun the flow, you should see a new session ID and a new
instance of the connector. The following example repeats the get-user-info operation
to demonstrate the creation and reuse of connections:

```
<?xml version="1.0" encoding="UTF-8"?>
<mule xmlns="http://www.mulesoft.org/schema/mule/core"
    xmlns:sfdc="http://www.mulesoft.org/schema/mule/sfdc"
    xmlns:http="http://www.mulesoft.org/schema/mule/http"
    xmlns:spring="http://www.springframework.org/schema/beans"
    xmlns:core="http://www.mulesoft.org/schema/mule/core"
    xmlns:xsi="http://www.w3.org/2001/XMLSchema-instance"
    xsi:schemaLocation="
        http://www.mulesoft.org/schema/mule/sfdc
        http://www.mulesoft.org/schema/mule/sfdc/current/mule-sfdc.xsd
        http://www.mulesoft.org/schema/mule/http
        http://www.mulesoft.org/schema/mule/http/current/mule-http.xsd
        http://www.springframework.org/schema/beans
        http://www.springframework.org/schema/beans/spring-beans-current.xsd
        http://www.mulesoft.org/schema/mule/core
        http://www.mulesoft.org/schema/mule/core/current/mule.xsd">

    <sfdc:config name="salesforce" />

    <flow name="salesforceSession">
        <http:inbound-endpoint host="localhost" port="8081"
            path="salesforce" />

        <sfdc:get-user-info username="bob"
            password="${salesforce.password}" securityToken="${salesforce.securi
tyToken}"
            config-ref="salesforce" />

        <sfdc:get-user-info username="ryan"
            password="${salesforce.password}" securityToken="${salesforce.securi
tyToken}"
            config-ref="salesforce" />

        <sfdc:get-user-info username="bob"
            password="${salesforce.password}" securityToken="${salesforce.securi
```

```
        tyToken}"
                config-ref="salesforce" />
        </flow>
    </mule>
```

The first invocation of the connector passes in the user bob, and as discussed this will create a new connector with the key bob and add it to the pool. It will first call the connect method and then execute the operation.

On the second invocation of the connector, the user passed in is ryan. In this case, Mule will check the connector pool to look for the key ryan and not find one, so it will create a new instance of the connector, add it to the pool with the key ryan, call the connect method, and execute the operation.

The third invocation reuses the connection key bob. When Mule checks the pool this time, it will find an instance of bob and reuse that connector. It will not call the connect method, but instead just execute the message processor and then return it to the pool. This is where the example becomes more efficient than the earlier ones. Because it is already connected, it can omit connecting to the service and retrieving a session key, and instead just use the session key from the previous invocation.

Fine-Tuning the Pool

Connection management is handled for you by default, but under some circumstances you might want to tune connection pooling to meet your organizational requirements. Salesforce allows administrators to configure the amount of user sessions, specify timeout values, impose restrictions on the maximum amount of API calls per day or per user, and so on.

For these types of circumstances, and to enable fine-tuning of the pool, the user of the connector can configure the pool by adding a connection-pooling-profile to the connector configuration, as shown in Example 5-3. This enables the user to configure the maximum amount of user sessions that can run concurrently, how long a session can be idle, etc.

Example 5-3. Fine-tuning a connector's connection pool

```
<?xml version="1.0" encoding="UTF-8"?>
<mule xmlns="http://www.mulesoft.org/schema/mule/core"
    xmlns:sfdc="http://www.mulesoft.org/schema/mule/sfdc"
    xmlns:http="http://www.mulesoft.org/schema/mule/http"
    xmlns:spring="http://www.springframework.org/schema/beans"
    xmlns:core="http://www.mulesoft.org/schema/mule/core"
    xmlns:xsi="http://www.w3.org/2001/XMLSchema-instance"
    xsi:schemaLocation="
        http://www.mulesoft.org/schema/mule/sfdc
        http://www.mulesoft.org/schema/mule/sfdc/current/mule-sfdc.xsd
        http://www.mulesoft.org/schema/mule/http
        http://www.mulesoft.org/schema/mule/http/current/mule-http.xsd
```

```
            http://www.springframework.org/schema/beans
            http://www.springframework.org/schema/beans/spring-beans-current.xsd
            http://www.mulesoft.org/schema/mule/core
            http://www.mulesoft.org/schema/mule/core/current/mule.xsd">

    <sfdc:config name="salesforce"
        username="${salesforce.username}" password="${salesforce.password}"
        securityToken="${salesforce.securityToken}">
        <sfdc:connection-pooling-profile
            maxActive="10" maxIdle="10"
            exhaustedAction="WHEN_EXHAUSTED_GROW" maxWait="120" />
    </sfdc:config>

    <flow name="salesforceSession">
        <http:inbound-endpoint host="localhost" port="8081"
            path="salesforce" />

        <sfdc:get-user-info config-ref="salesforce" />
    </flow>
</mule>
```

A connector's pooling profile configures its component pool. The most important setting is maxActive, which specifies the maximum number of instances of the connector
that Mule will create to handle simultaneous requests. When maxActive is exceeded,
the pool is said to be *exhausted*. The full list of configuration follows:

exhaustedAction

Specifies the behavior of the Mule component pool when the pool is exhausted.
Possible values are WHEN_EXHAUSTED_FAIL (throws a NoSuchElementException
when you already are using the maximum number of sessions), WHEN_EXHAUS
TED_WAIT (blocks by invoking Object.wait(long) until a new or idle object is
available), and WHEN_EXHAUSTED_GROW (creates a new Mule instance and returns it,
essentially making maxActive meaningless). If a positive maxWait value is supplied,
it will block for at most that many milliseconds, after which a NoSuchElementEx
ception will be thrown. A negative maxThreadWait will block indefinitely.

initialisationPolicy

Determines how components in a pool should be initialized. The possible values
are INITIALISE_NONE (will not load any components into the pool on startup),
INITIALISE_ONE (will load one initial component into the pool on startup), and
INITIALISE_ALL (will load all components in the pool on startup).

maxActive

Controls the maximum number of Mule components that can be borrowed from a
session at one time. When set to a negative value, there is no limit to the number
of components that may be active at one time.

maxWait
> Specifies the number of milliseconds to wait for a pooled component to become available when the pool is exhausted and the `exhaustedAction` is set to `WHEN_EX HAUSTED_WAIT`.

Reconnection Strategies

Reconnection strategies specify how a connector behaves when its connection fails. Some connectors offer automatic retries for certain operations. There are a couple of situations in which a retry may solve the problem at hand—for example, if the system is currently busy or if the session has expired.

One situation that can produce problems involves timeouts. For example, an administrator of a Salesforce.com organization can set the session timeout for their users. This session timeout setting is not exposed through the API, which makes it difficult to predict whether the session ID for a connection that you haven't used for a while is still valid. So if a connection is left idle, calling the API using an idle session ID will result in an error. A new session key needs to be retrieved and the API operation retried.

On top of timeouts, not only can another application logging in with the same user account kill your session by calling `logout()`, it can also keep your session ID valid by using the API when your application is idle.

These kinds of situations are solvable by reacquiring a connection and retrying the operation. Cloud Connectors will automatically detect invalid session ID errors, and allow you to log in again, retrieve a new session, and retry the operation. They allow you to customize and better control the behavior of a failed connection, by specifying a number of criteria such as:

- The type of exception
- The number and frequency of reconnection attempts
- The notifications generated, and more

In order to configure this functionality, Mule provides a set of three reconnection strategies. Each reconnection strategy can be configured as a child element of a connector's global `config` declaration. The following sections detail how to configure each reconnection strategy. More information on available and custom reconnection strategies can be found here (*http://bit.ly/1nfB6uM*).

Reconnection strategies were previously called retry policies and were an EE (Enterprise Edition)-only feature. Since Mule version 3.3.0, the feature was also made available to CE (Community Edition) users as well, which means that CE Cloud Connectors like Salesforce can take advantage of these features. Prior to this, Cloud Connectors had their own implementation of reconnection strategies via a `retryMax` attribute at the operation level:

```
<sfdc:get-session-id retryMax="5" config-ref="salesforce" />
```

The `retryMax` argument specifies how many times the specific operation should be retried. The operation is only retried under known conditions specified by the developer of the connector and isn't open to customization by the end user of the connector. This functionality has since been deprecated in favor of the common Mule reconnection strategies.

Standard Reconnection Strategy

The standard reconnection strategy, `reconnect`, is a reconnection strategy that allows the user to configure how many times a reconnection should be attempted and how long to wait between attempts. Example 5-4 demonstrates configuring a standard reconnection strategy to define how many times a reconnection should be attempted and the frequency between each attempt.

Example 5-4. Standard reconnection strategy

```
<?xml version="1.0" encoding="UTF-8"?>
<mule xmlns="http://www.mulesoft.org/schema/mule/core"
    xmlns:sfdc="http://www.mulesoft.org/schema/mule/sfdc"
    xmlns:http="http://www.mulesoft.org/schema/mule/http"
    xmlns:spring="http://www.springframework.org/schema/beans"
    xmlns:core="http://www.mulesoft.org/schema/mule/core"
    xmlns:xsi="http://www.w3.org/2001/XMLSchema-instance"
    xsi:schemaLocation="
        http://www.mulesoft.org/schema/mule/sfdc
        http://www.mulesoft.org/schema/mule/sfdc/current/mule-sfdc.xsd
        http://www.mulesoft.org/schema/mule/http
        http://www.mulesoft.org/schema/mule/http/current/mule-http.xsd
        http://www.springframework.org/schema/beans
        http://www.springframework.org/schema/beans/spring-beans-current.xsd
        http://www.mulesoft.org/schema/mule/core
        http://www.mulesoft.org/schema/mule/core/current/mule.xsd">

    <sfdc:config name="salesforce"
        username="${salesforce.username}" password="${salesforce.password}"
        securityToken="${salesforce.securityToken}">
        <reconnect count="5" frequency="1000" />
    </sfdc:config>
```

```
<flow name="salesforceSession">
    <http:inbound-endpoint host="localhost" port="8081"
        path="salesforce" />

    <sfdc:get-user-info config-ref="salesforce" />
</flow>
</mule>
```

This example amends the previous configuration to use the standard `reconnect` strategy. The most important setting here is the `count` attribute that defines how many times a reconnection should be attempted. The full list of configuration follows:

blocking
> A boolean value to determine whether the reconnection strategy will run in the current thread or if false, run in a separate, non-blocking thread

frequency
> How often (in milliseconds) to wait between reconnection attempts

count
> How many times a reconnection should be attempted

Using the current configuration, the connector will retry up to a maximum of five times and at a frequency of one second using the `count` and `frequency` attributes, respectively. If for any reason a session becomes invalid or the service becomes unavailable, the operation will now attempt to retry the operation up to five times before eventually throwing an exception if unsuccessful.

Reconnect Forever Strategy

The reconnect forever strategy, `reconnect-forever`, is a reconnection strategy that retries an infinite number of times at the specified frequency. This strategy is very similar to the previous `reconnect` strategy, but with the subtle difference of not setting a `count` attribute to limit the maximum amount of retries. Example 5-5 demonstrates this approach.

Example 5-5. Reconnect forever strategy

```
<?xml version="1.0" encoding="UTF-8"?>
<mule xmlns="http://www.mulesoft.org/schema/mule/core"
    xmlns:sfdc="http://www.mulesoft.org/schema/mule/sfdc"
    xmlns:http="http://www.mulesoft.org/schema/mule/http"
    xmlns:spring="http://www.springframework.org/schema/beans"
    xmlns:core="http://www.mulesoft.org/schema/mule/core"
    xmlns:xsi="http://www.w3.org/2001/XMLSchema-instance"
    xsi:schemaLocation="
        http://www.mulesoft.org/schema/mule/sfdc
        http://www.mulesoft.org/schema/mule/sfdc/current/mule-sfdc.xsd
        http://www.mulesoft.org/schema/mule/http
```

```
        http://www.mulesoft.org/schema/mule/http/current/mule-http.xsd
        http://www.springframework.org/schema/beans
        http://www.springframework.org/schema/beans/spring-beans-current.xsd
        http://www.mulesoft.org/schema/mule/core
        http://www.mulesoft.org/schema/mule/core/current/mule.xsd">

    <sfdc:config name="salesforce"
        username="${salesforce.username}" password="${salesforce.password}"
        securityToken="${salesforce.securityToken}">
        <reconnect-forever frequency="1000" />
    </sfdc:config>

    <flow name="salesforceSession">
        <http:inbound-endpoint host="localhost" port="8081"
            path="salesforce" />

        <sfdc:get-user-info config-ref="salesforce" />
    </flow>
</mule>
```

This example amends the previous configuration to use the reconnect-forever strategy. The most important setting here is the frequency attribute that defines how long to wait between reconnection attempts. This configuration no longer requires the count attribute as it will retry indefinitely. The full list of configuration follows:

blocking
> A boolean value to determine whether the reconnection strategy will run in the current thread or if false, run in a separate, non-blocking thread

frequency
> How often (in milliseconds) to wait between reconnection attempts

Custom Reconnection Strategy

The custom reconnection strategy, reconnect-custom-strategy, is a custom, user-defined reconnection strategy that allows you to take specific action based on the type of exception and decide whether or not the connection should be retried. Example 5-6 demonstrates this approach.

Example 5-6. Custom reconnection strategy

```
<?xml version="1.0" encoding="UTF-8"?>
<mule xmlns="http://www.mulesoft.org/schema/mule/core"
    xmlns:sfdc="http://www.mulesoft.org/schema/mule/sfdc"
    xmlns:http="http://www.mulesoft.org/schema/mule/http"
    xmlns:spring="http://www.springframework.org/schema/beans"
    xmlns:core="http://www.mulesoft.org/schema/mule/core"
    xmlns:xsi="http://www.w3.org/2001/XMLSchema-instance"
    xsi:schemaLocation="
        http://www.mulesoft.org/schema/mule/sfdc
        http://www.mulesoft.org/schema/mule/sfdc/current/mule-sfdc.xsd
```

```
           http://www.mulesoft.org/schema/mule/http
           http://www.mulesoft.org/schema/mule/http/current/mule-http.xsd
           http://www.springframework.org/schema/beans
           http://www.springframework.org/schema/beans/spring-beans-current.xsd
           http://www.mulesoft.org/schema/mule/core
           http://www.mulesoft.org/schema/mule/core/current/mule.xsd">

    <sfdc:config name="salesforce"
        username="${salesforce.username}" password="${salesforce.password}"
        securityToken="${salesforce.securityToken}">
        <reconnect-custom-strategy
            class="org.mule.retry.policies.NoRetryPolicyTemplate" />
    </sfdc:config>

    <flow name="salesforceSession">
        <http:inbound-endpoint host="localhost" port="8081"
            path="salesforce" />

        <sfdc:get-user-info config-ref="salesforce" />
    </flow>
</mule>
```

This example amends the previous configuration to use the `reconnect-custom-strategy`. The most important setting here is the `class` attribute that references a class that implements the `org.mule.api.retry.RetryPolicy` interface. The full list of configuration follows:

blocking
> A boolean value to determine whether the reconnection strategy will run in the current thread or if false, run in a separate, non-blocking thread

class
> A class that implements the `org.mule.api.retry.RetryPolicy` interface

Example 5-7 demonstrates a basic class implementing the `org.mule.api.retry.Ret ryPolicy` interface, where the method `PolicyStatus applyPolicy(Throwable cause)` takes some action based on the type of exception, then returns `PolicyStatus` to indicate whether the policy has been exhausted or should continue to retry. This particular implementation does not attempt a retry at all, and merely acts as a placeholder to demonstrate.

Example 5-7. Custom retry policy

```
package org.mule.retry.policies;

import org.mule.api.retry.RetryPolicy;
import org.mule.retry.PolicyStatus;

/**
 * This policy is basically a placeholder.  It does not attempt to retry at all.
 */
```

```
public class NoRetryPolicyTemplate extends AbstractPolicyTemplate
{
    public RetryPolicy createRetryInstance()
    {
        return new NoRetryPolicy();
    }

    protected static class NoRetryPolicy implements RetryPolicy
    {
        public PolicyStatus applyPolicy(Throwable cause)
        {
            return PolicyStatus.policyExhausted(cause);
        }
    }

    public String toString()
    {
        return "NoRetryPolicy{}";
    }
}
```

Summary

In this chapter we have briefly discussed stateful APIs and session-based authentication. Building your own connection management around these APIs can be tricky, to say the least: creating and managing your own connection pools, detecting idle sessions, and retrying operations. Cloud Connectors abstract this away, providing a consistent interface for fine-tuning yourself—and finally, no more session drop-outs!

CHAPTER 6

Real-Time Connectivity and Synchronization

We can all agree that APIs are great. They open up silos to a wealth of data and functionality, but the vast majority of these Web APIs use the HTTP request-response model, requiring the client to make a request to a server and wait for a response in an interactive fashion. This is fine for the majority of our examples so far, such as sending a Tweet, adding a contact, etc. But what about when you actively want to retrieve updates about a particular resource, such as who's talking about my company on Twitter today? You wouldn't have someone sitting there issuing a request every 5 minutes would you? No, ideally you want to be notified in a real-time fashion when someone is talking about your company or when something happens to your account.

One traditional solution is polling, whereby a request with your particular search terms is scheduled to periodically call an API, process the response, and then repeat. This results, however, in developers calling these APIs over and over again to get updates, only to find out nothing has changed. This process constantly uses up resources and is not acceptable to either the API consumer or the API provider. If you're just using Twitter to see what your friends are chatting about, then waiting 30 seconds to a minute to call the API and filter out the duplicate messages might be fine, but if you're relying on these APIs for sales leads or financial data, then polling just won't do. This is where "real-time" technologies come in.

Take AJAX for example. We have had technologies enabling real-time events for the frontend for years, but on the backend we still revert to polling these Web APIs in request-response style. Polling an API isn't the worst thing in the world and may be the only option in some cases. But not only is it inefficient to constantly ask an API for changes, it encounters the rate limiting imposed by most open APIs. They often restrict the number of calls a single account can issue to them a day, meaning you cannot even get close to real time without paying for it. Polling is the API equivalent of the child in the back seat constantly asking "Are we there yet?" only to get the same response, and there's only so long before the driver stops responding.

Real-time needs to run on APIs as much as it runs inside a web browser. There are already technologies and trends leading us towards real-time data, including push technologies such as WebHooks and streaming APIs. The efficiency offered by push technologies is shown in Figure 6-1. This chapter will take a look at traditional polling mechanisms and demonstrate, by example, how Cloud Connectors simplify using these newer technologies and the benefits of using these technologies with some of the most popular open APIs.

Polling Connectors

To demonstrate the benefits of "push versus pull" in action, let's first take a look at an example polling application. For this example, we will use one of the Twitter request-response style APIs. Twitter provides an API for their search facility and can be invoked by the Mule Twitter connector through the aptly named `search` operation.

A Polling Operation

As a basic start, we'll do a search that drags in all results as a single response, as shown in Example 6-1.

Example 6-1. Twitter polling example

```
<?xml version="1.0" encoding="UTF-8"?>
<mule xmlns="http://www.mulesoft.org/schema/mule/core"
    xmlns:http="http://www.mulesoft.org/schema/mule/http"
    xmlns:twitter="http://www.mulesoft.org/schema/mule/twitter"
    xmlns:spring="http://www.springframework.org/schema/beans"
    xmlns:xsi="http://www.w3.org/2001/XMLSchema-instance"
    xsi:schemaLocation="
        http://www.mulesoft.org/schema/mule/http
        http://www.mulesoft.org/schema/mule/http/current/mule-http.xsd
        http://www.mulesoft.org/schema/mule/twitter
        http://www.mulesoft.org/schema/mule/twitter/current/mule-twitter.xsd
        http://www.springframework.org/schema/beans
        http://www.springframework.org/schema/beans/spring-beans-3.0.xsd
        http://www.mulesoft.org/schema/mule/core
        http://www.mulesoft.org/schema/mule/core/current/mule.xsd">

    <twitter:config name="twitter" consumerKey="${twitter.consumer.key}"
        consumerSecret="${twitter.consumer.secret}"
        accessKey="${twitter.access.key}"
        accessSecret="${twitter.access.secret}" />

    <flow name="twitterPolling">
        <poll frequency="30000">
            <twitter:search query="mule" />
```

```
        </poll>

        <logger message="#[payload]" level="INFO" />
    </flow>
</mule>
```

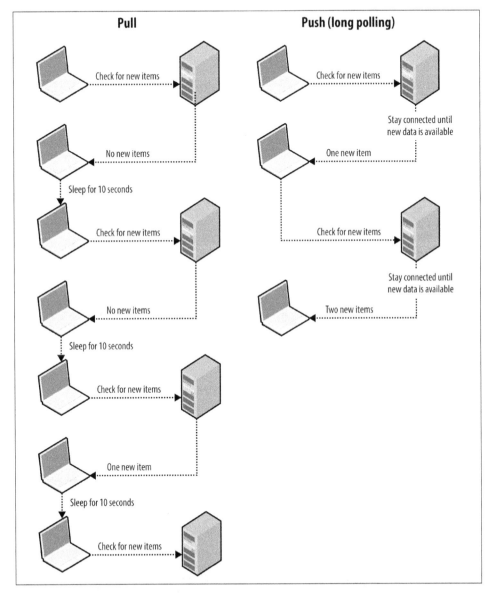

Figure 6-1. Visualization of push versus pull

In this example, we have first defined our Twitter `search` operation within a `poll` element. The `poll` element can be used in place of an inbound endpoint and can poll any message processor, using the result as the source of a flow. This configuration will automatically invoke the search operation based on the `frequency` attribute (in milliseconds)—in this case, every 5 minutes (30,000 milliseconds). Secondly, within the `search` operation we are defining just one attribute named `query` and the value is just the term we want to search for—in this case, `mule`.

Parsing the Response

After querying the search API, we need to work with the search results. As we have set the `config` element `format` attribute to `JSON`, the response format will be a JSON-formatted array of search results similar to the output in Example 6-2.

Example 6-2. Example JSON output from Twitter search API

```
{"results":[
    {"text":"@twitterapi  http:\/\/tinyurl.com\/ctrefg",
     "to_user_id":396524,
     "to_user":"TwitterAPI",
     "from_user":"jkoum",
     "id":1478555574,
     "from_user_id":1833773,
     "iso_language_code":"nl",
     "source":"<a href="http:\/\/twitter.com\/">
            twitter<\/a>",
            "profile_image_url":"http:\/\/...\/2522215727_a5f07da155_b_normal.jpg",
            "created_at":"Wed, 08 Apr 2009 19:22:10 +0000"}],
            "since_id":0,
            "max_id":1480307926,
            "refresh_url":"?since_id=1480307926&q=%40twitterapi",
            "results_per_page":15,
            "next_page":"?page=2&max_id=1480307926&q=%40twitterapi",
            "completed_in":0.031704,
            "page":1,
            "query":"%40twitterapi"
    },
    {"text":"@twitterapi  http:\/\/tinyurl.com\/ctrefg",
     "to_user_id":396524,
     "to_user":"TwitterAPI",
     "from_user":"jkoum",
     "id":1478555574,
     "from_user_id":1833773,
     "iso_language_code":"nl",
     "source":"<a href="http:\/\/twitter.com\/">
            twitter<\/a>",
            "profile_image_url":"http:\/\/...\/2522215727_a5f07da155_b_normal.jpg",
            "created_at":"Wed, 08 Apr 2009 19:22:10 +0000"}],
            "since_id":0,
            "max_id":1480307926,
```

```
            "refresh_url":"?since_id=1480307926&q=%40twitterapi",
            "results_per_page":15,
            "next_page":"?page=2&max_id=1480307926&q=%40twitterapi",
            "completed_in":0.031704,
            "page":1,
            "query":"%40twitterapi"
        }
]}
```

This response has been shortened for brevity. But as you can see, it is a JSON-formatted array of Tweets named `results` (indicated by the [and] characters that represent JSON arrays).

Splitting things up

To work with these Tweets individually, we can split the response into multiple Tweets using the `splitter` element.

Example 6-3 amends the previous example to split the Twitter search response into individual Tweets, passing in the expression #[payload.tweets], which represents the collection to split, so that the splitter knows it should split this array into its individual entries.

Example 6-3. Twitter splitting example

```xml
<?xml version="1.0" encoding="UTF-8"?>
<mule xmlns="http://www.mulesoft.org/schema/mule/core"
    xmlns:http="http://www.mulesoft.org/schema/mule/http"
    xmlns:twitter="http://www.mulesoft.org/schema/mule/twitter"
    xmlns:spring="http://www.springframework.org/schema/beans"
    xmlns:xsi="http://www.w3.org/2001/XMLSchema-instance"
    xsi:schemaLocation="
        http://www.mulesoft.org/schema/mule/http
        http://www.mulesoft.org/schema/mule/http/current/mule-http.xsd
        http://www.mulesoft.org/schema/mule/twitter
        http://www.mulesoft.org/schema/mule/twitter/current/mule-twitter.xsd
        http://www.springframework.org/schema/beans
        http://www.springframework.org/schema/beans/spring-beans-3.0.xsd
        http://www.mulesoft.org/schema/mule/core
        http://www.mulesoft.org/schema/mule/core/current/mule.xsd">

    <twitter:config name="twitter" consumerKey="${twitter.consumer.key}"
        consumerSecret="${twitter.consumer.secret}"
        accessKey="${twitter.access.key}"
        accessSecret="${twitter.access.secret}" />

    <flow name="twitterPolling">
        <poll frequency="30000">
            <twitter:search query="mule" />
        </poll>
```

```
        <splitter expression="#[payload.tweets]" />

        <logger message="#[payload]" level="INFO" />
    </flow>
</mule>
```

Filtering unique results

One particular criticism of polling is that repeatedly querying the same API within short
spaces of time will result in the majority of results being duplicates. For these types of
situations, Mule provides a handy way to filter unique results via an `idempotent-
message-filter`. An idempotent message filter checks a user-defined unique ID of the
incoming message to ensure that only unique messages continue processing.
Example 6-4 demonstrates using an `idempotent-message-filter` to filter unique
Tweets.

Example 6-4. Filtering unique Tweets

```
<?xml version="1.0" encoding="UTF-8"?>
<mule xmlns="http://www.mulesoft.org/schema/mule/core"
    xmlns:http="http://www.mulesoft.org/schema/mule/http"
    xmlns:twitter="http://www.mulesoft.org/schema/mule/twitter"
    xmlns:spring="http://www.springframework.org/schema/beans"
    xmlns:xsi="http://www.w3.org/2001/XMLSchema-instance"
    xsi:schemaLocation="
        http://www.mulesoft.org/schema/mule/http
        http://www.mulesoft.org/schema/mule/http/current/mule-http.xsd
        http://www.mulesoft.org/schema/mule/twitter
        http://www.mulesoft.org/schema/mule/twitter/current/mule-twitter.xsd
        http://www.springframework.org/schema/beans
        http://www.springframework.org/schema/beans/spring-beans-3.0.xsd
        http://www.mulesoft.org/schema/mule/core
        http://www.mulesoft.org/schema/mule/core/current/mule.xsd">

    <twitter:config name="twitter" consumerKey="${twitter.consumer.key}"
        consumerSecret="${twitter.consumer.secret}"
        accessKey="${twitter.access.key}"
        accessSecret="${twitter.access.secret}" />

    <flow name="twitterPolling">
        <poll frequency="30000">
            <twitter:search query="mule" />
        </poll>

        <splitter expression="#[payload.tweets]" />

        <idempotent-message-filter idExpression="#[payload.id]" />

        <logger message="#[payload]" level="INFO" />
    </flow>
</mule>
```

After splitting the results, the example now uses an `idempotent-message-filter` element, setting one sole attribute: `idExpression`. This attribute defines how to generate the unique identifier of a message in order to compare uniqueness based on Mule expressions. In this case, we are using a MEL expression to extract the Tweet ID using `#[payload.id]`.

Fine-Grained Scheduling

The poll element we used in the previous example is very useful for executing simple tasks at specific intervals, but when you need to deal with more complex, finer-grained synchronisation cycles, it simply isn't up to the task. Fortunately, the `poll` element provides another facility for scheduling via `schedulers`.

Fixed frequency scheduler

As the name suggests, this scheduler allows you to configure a polling schedule at a fixed frequency. You may be wondering how this is different from the `frequency` attribute on the `poll` element previously. Well, it's both similar and confusing. But what this scheduler gives you is the ability to provide a much more precise scheduling frequency. The `frequency` attribute previously takes only millisecond values and starts polling immediately. The new `fixed-frequency-scheduler` gives you additional attributes to fine tune your polling frequency. Example 6-5 demonstrates the new features.

Example 6-5. Twitter fixed frequency scheduling

```
<?xml version="1.0" encoding="UTF-8"?>
<mule xmlns="http://www.mulesoft.org/schema/mule/core"
    xmlns:twitter="http://www.mulesoft.org/schema/mule/twitter"
    xmlns:spring="http://www.springframework.org/schema/beans"
    xmlns:xsi="http://www.w3.org/2001/XMLSchema-instance"
    xsi:schemaLocation="
        http://www.mulesoft.org/schema/mule/http
        http://www.mulesoft.org/schema/mule/http/current/mule-http.xsd
        http://www.mulesoft.org/schema/mule/twitter
        http://www.mulesoft.org/schema/mule/twitter/current/mule-twitter.xsd
        http://www.springframework.org/schema/beans
        http://www.springframework.org/schema/beans/spring-beans-3.0.xsd
        http://www.mulesoft.org/schema/mule/core
        http://www.mulesoft.org/schema/mule/core/current/mule.xsd">

    <twitter:config name="twitter" consumerKey="${twitter.consumer.key}"
        consumerSecret="${twitter.consumer.secret}"
        accessKey="${twitter.access.key}"
        accessSecret="${twitter.access.secret}" />

    <flow name="twitterFixedScheduling">
        <poll>
                <fixed-frequency-scheduler frequency="10" timeUnit="MINUTES" startDe
lay="1" />
```

```
        <twitter:search query="mule" />
    </poll>

    <logger message="#[payload]" level="INFO" />
    </flow>
</mule>
```

As you can see, we have removed the `frequency` attribute and added an additional `fixed-frequency-scheduler` element to our `poll` element. The following list details the new attributes and how we have configured them:

frequency
> Just like the previous `frequency` attribute, this allows you to configure the polling frequency; unlike before, this now works in tandem with a specific `timeUnit`.

startDelay
> This attribute allows you stall the execution of the poll on its very first run, where as previously the poll would start imminently. Note that the value for this is also expressed in the same time unit as the frequency.

So with these values in place, our poll will now run every ten minutes, but will wait one minute before its very first poll. This simplifies scheduling dramatically, and the scheduler support is relatively new (just imagine how ugly this was previously trying to express one day in milliseconds).

Cron scheduler

As the name implies, this scheduler allows you to configure a polling schedule using cron expressions. A cron expression is a string comprised of six or seven fields separated by white space. Fields can contain any of the allowed values, along with various combinations of the allowed special characters for that field. Cron expressions can be as simple as this:

```
* * * * ? *
```

or more complex, like this:

```
0 0/5 14,18,3-39,52 ? JAN,MAR,SEP MON-FRI 2002-2010.
```

Example 6-6 will generate a job every five minutes as before and trigger our flow, which will in turn call the Twitter connector as before.

Example 6-6. Twitter scheduling

```
<?xml version="1.0" encoding="UTF-8"?>
<mule xmlns="http://www.mulesoft.org/schema/mule/core"
    xmlns:twitter="http://www.mulesoft.org/schema/mule/twitter"
    xmlns:schedulers="http://www.mulesoft.org/schema/mule/schedulers"
    xmlns:spring="http://www.springframework.org/schema/beans"
    xmlns:xsi="http://www.w3.org/2001/XMLSchema-instance"
    xsi:schemaLocation="
```

```
            http://www.mulesoft.org/schema/mule/http
            http://www.mulesoft.org/schema/mule/http/current/mule-http.xsd
            http://www.mulesoft.org/schema/mule/twitter
            http://www.mulesoft.org/schema/mule/twitter/current/mule-twitter.xsd
            http://www.mulesoft.org/schema/mule/schedulers
            http://www.mulesoft.org/schema/mule/schedulers/current/mule-schedulers.xsd
            http://www.springframework.org/schema/beans
            http://www.springframework.org/schema/beans/spring-beans-3.0.xsd
            http://www.mulesoft.org/schema/mule/core
            http://www.mulesoft.org/schema/mule/core/current/mule.xsd">

    <twitter:config name="twitter" consumerKey="${twitter.consumer.key}"
        consumerSecret="${twitter.consumer.secret}"
        accessKey="${twitter.access.key}"
        accessSecret="${twitter.access.secret}" />

    <flow name="twitterCronScheduling">
        <poll>
            <schedulers:cron-scheduler expression="0 0/5 * * ?" />
            <twitter:search query="mule" />
        </poll>

        <logger message="#[payload]" level="INFO" />
    </flow>
</mule>
```

Watermarking

The term *watermarking* is borrowed from floods, whereby you measure the watermarks on a surface to see how high the water rose. This resonates with data synchronization when you need to measure how much of a particular dataset you have already processed.

In our previous examples, we poll the Twitter API each time to look for new data and filter out previously processed records. However, this is not advantageous when you are working with massive datasets and have to wade through the ones we have previously processed each time. This is where the concept of watermarking can help. Watermarking allows us to pick up from where we last left off without having to reprocess and filter out the old data that we do not care about anymore.

It sounds reasonably straightforward to pick up from where we last left off; however, we must generate a marker such as a timestamp or the last ID processed, persist the marker between polls, update the marker after each poll, and handle any errors to ensure no data is missed. This logic is quite complicated and verbose to take care of manually. Luckily, Mule provides a special watermark processor that will automatically handle all of this for us.

If you look back at the response form the Twitter search operation in Example 6-2, you will notice that each Tweet contains a sinceId attribute. The Twitter connector allows us to set this on the search operation to only return results with an ID greater than (that is, more recent than) the specified ID. We will use this as our marker so that new polls pick up only from the last ID we processed. Example 6-2 amends the previous example to include the watermarking process.

Example 6-7. Twitter watermarking

```xml
<?xml version="1.0" encoding="UTF-8"?>
<mule xmlns="http://www.mulesoft.org/schema/mule/core"
    xmlns:http="http://www.mulesoft.org/schema/mule/http"
    xmlns:twitter="http://www.mulesoft.org/schema/mule/twitter"
    xmlns:spring="http://www.springframework.org/schema/beans"
    xmlns:xsi="http://www.w3.org/2001/XMLSchema-instance"
    xsi:schemaLocation="
        http://www.mulesoft.org/schema/mule/http
        http://www.mulesoft.org/schema/mule/http/current/mule-http.xsd
        http://www.mulesoft.org/schema/mule/twitter
        http://www.mulesoft.org/schema/mule/twitter/current/mule-twitter.xsd
        http://www.springframework.org/schema/beans
        http://www.springframework.org/schema/beans/spring-beans-3.0.xsd
        http://www.mulesoft.org/schema/mule/core
        http://www.mulesoft.org/schema/mule/core/current/mule.xsd ">

    <twitter:config name="twitter" consumerKey="${twitter.consumer.key}"
        consumerSecret="${twitter.consumer.secret}"
        accessKey="${twitter.access.key}"
        accessSecret="${twitter.access.secret}" />

    <flow name="twitterWatermarking"> processingStrategy="synchronous"
        <poll frequency="30000">
            <watermark variable="lastId" default-expression="#[0]"
                update-expression="#[payload.sinceId]" />
                <twitter:search query="mule" sinceId="#[flowVars["lastId"]]" />
        </poll>

            <logger message="#[payload]" level="INFO" />
    </flow>
</mule>
```

As you can see, the poll element now includes a watermark element. The following list describes each attribute in detail:

variable

This attribute defines the name of the variable that will be used to store our marker. In this case, the variable is lastId.

default-expression

This attribute is used to define the default value for this variable. On our very fist poll, there will be no marker stored so we need to provide a default one. As we will be using the Twitter sinceId, which is numeric, we set this to 0 because all Tweets will have an ID greater than 0.

update-expression

> This attribute is used to extract the marker from the data we are processing. As we are interested in the `sinceId` attribute from each Tweet, we set the value to `pay load.sinceId`. Note that if we executed this expression directly on the Twitter search response, it would fail since the response is a collection of Tweets. However, the watermark processor is clever enough to work this out for us by automatically inspecting each in object in the collection.

After the watermark is defined, you will notice that we have amended the Twitter `search` operation to include the `sinceId` attribute and set its value to choose the `lastId` variable that we previously stored in the watermark. On running this flow, you will see that the first poll will search for Tweets with an ID greater than 0 and subsequent polls will only search for Tweets with an ID greater than the last one we processed.

By using the watermark processor, Mule takes care of persisting your marker between polls in its internal object store, which we discussed in Chapter 4. It takes care of checking if a watermark value already exists, it automatically gets the next value, and it will update the value when the poll is complete (or instead, leave it untouched if it fails).

 The `flow` now has an additional attribute named `processingStrat egy`. Processing strategies in Mule allow you configure the synchronicity and threading profiles of various elements in your Mule applications. The `>watermark` processor dictates that you use the "synchronous" processing strategy as detailed in the previous example. More information on processing strategies can be found in the Flow Processing Strategies documentation (*http://bit.ly/1nfBeue*).

Streaming APIs

Now we can turn to the newer push methods of real-time querying. Typically, when you think of streaming protocols, video or audio streaming may come to mind, but many service providers out there are also offering this functionality for their application data. Salesforce, Facebook, Twitter, and many more services are now provide streaming APIs as a way of delivering their data to clients in a real-time fashion.

Streaming APIs still use the HTTP protocol, but instead of responding to a request with a single piece of data, the server responds with a continuous stream of updates as soon as they are available. These are real-time notifications on any given event on which you want to trigger some operation.

There is currently no standard or consistent approach to building or consuming streaming APIs. The different approaches include:

HTTP using long poll

Long poll is a variation of the traditional polling technique, emulating an information push from a server to a client. This method is used by some HTTP servers to hold a connection open for a client until data becomes available on the server. The client sends a poll at regular but infrequent intervals. If the server has data available, it sends the data in response to the client request. If not, instead of sending an empty response, the server holds the request and waits for some information to be available.

Comet over HTTP

Comet is a server-side pub-sub implementation designed around the Bayeux protocol (*http://cometd.org/documentation/bayeux*), which is often used to enable AJAX capabilities on Java servers. Comet is stateful, maintaining a session between client and server.

HTTP server push

HTTP server push is the most common technique associated with HTTP streaming. HTTP server push can send data from a web server to a web browser via several mechanisms. Using these techniques, a web server does not terminate a connection after pushing data to a client, but instead keeps the connection open so that if another event is received, it can immediately be sent to the client.

With multiple techniques and no consistent approach, coupled with the fact that HTTP streaming doesn't work quite the same way most HTTP-based services work, the program that reads the stream has to be written to process the incoming data, handle reconnects, and so on, resulting in a much higher entry barrier for programmers.

Cloud Connectors abstract away all this complexity and instead provide a consistent approach to consuming these types of APIs, lowering the entry barrier for programmers.

Configuring Streaming Connectors

To show streaming connectors in action, we'll stick with Twitter. Twitter provides various streaming APIs that allow high throughput near real-time access to various subsets of public and protected Twitter data. In turn, the Mule Twitter connector provides various operations for easily working with these APIs:

twitter:filtered-stream

Asynchronously retrieves public statuses that match one or more filter predicates.

twitter:firehose-stream

Asynchronously retrieves all public statuses.

twitter:link-stream

Asynchronously retrieves all statuses containing `http:` and `https:` prefixes.

twitter:sample-stream
 Asynchronously retrieves a random sample of all public statuses.

twitter:site-stream
 Asynchronously retrieves statutes for a set of supplied user IDs.

Consuming the Stream

All Cloud Connector operations thus far have been "message processors." As discussed in "Message Sources" on page 7, a message processor can be used only after receiving a message from a message source, such as an inbound endpoint or a polling processor, and cannot be used at the beginning of a flow to trigger execution. The Twitter connector exposes many message processors for interacting with Twitter in this fashion, but as we want to use a streaming API, we don't need a separate message source. We just want the API call itself to be the source of the message. To accomplish this, streaming API operations are implemented as message sources themselves and not as message processors. This allows us to use them at the beginning of flows.

Let's start with the `filtered-stream` message source. Example 6-8 amends the Twitter polling example in Example 6-1 to use the Twitter-streaming API instead.

Example 6-8. Twitter-streaming example

```
<?xml version="1.0" encoding="UTF-8"?>
<mule xmlns="http://www.mulesoft.org/schema/mule/core"
    xmlns:twitter="http://www.mulesoft.org/schema/mule/twitter"
    xmlns:spring="http://www.springframework.org/schema/beans"
    xmlns:xsi="http://www.w3.org/2001/XMLSchema-instance"
    xsi:schemaLocation="
        http://www.mulesoft.org/schema/mule/twitter
        http://www.mulesoft.org/schema/mule/twitter/current/mule-twitter.xsd
        http://www.springframework.org/schema/beans
        http://www.springframework.org/schema/beans/spring-beans-3.0.xsd
        http://www.mulesoft.org/schema/mule/core
        http://www.mulesoft.org/schema/mule/core/current/mule.xsd ">

    <twitter:config name="twitter" consumerKey="${twitter.consumer.key}"
        consumerSecret="${twitter.consumer.secret}"
        accessKey="${twitter.access.key}"
        accessSecret="${twitter.access.secret}" />

    <flow name="twitterStreaming">
        <twitter:filtered-stream>
            <twitter:keywords>
                <twitter:keyword>mule</twitter:keyword>
            </twitter:keywords>
        </twitter:filtered-stream>

        <logger message="@#[payload.from_user] - #[payload.text]" level="INFO" />
```

```
    </flow>
</mule>
```

As discussed previously, we no longer need a separate message source such as a poll element because the operation is the source itself. The flow now starts with the `filtered-stream` element. This element has two optional child elements for defining the filters to use. Because we are amending the original example to search for the keyword `mule`, we are using the `twitter:keywords` filter. This is one of two possible filters. The other, `user-ids`, tracks updates associated with a particular Twitter user ID. The `twitter:keywords` element also has a child element, `twitter:keyword`, which sets the keyword we want to search for. You can use any number of keyword elements, but must provide at least one.

If you run this flow, it will now run continuously, consuming a filtered Twitter stream about the topic `mule` and log it to the console.

Parsing the Stream

The previous Twitter polling example in Example 6-1, after polling the search API, returned us a JSON-formatted array of Tweets, as shown in Example 6-2. This looks a little different in the streaming API. The JSON response will instead just be an individual object looking similar to the output in the following example response:

```
{"text":"RT @gillesguillemin: Google FINALLY Releases AS3 Player for YouTube
        http://bit.ly/yKgaz",
    "favorited":false,
    "in_reply_to_user_id":null,
    "in_reply_to_screen_name":null,
    "source":"web",
    "geo":null,
    "in_reply_to_status_id":null,
    "user":{
        "friends_count":52,
        "screen_name":"imrahil",
        "verified":false,
        "profile_background_color":"9ae4e8",
        "favourites_count":8,
        "notifications":null,
        "profile_text_color":"000000",
        "description":"",
        "location":"Poland",
        "time_zone":"Warsaw",
        "profile_link_color":"0000ff",
        "following":null,
        "profile_background_image_url":"http://s.twimg.com/a/1255558003/images/
                                themes/theme1/bg.png",
        "profile_sidebar_fill_color":"e0ff92",
        "protected":false,"url":"http://flex.imrahil.com",
        "geo_enabled":false,
```

```
            "profile_background_tile":false,
            "name":"Jarek",
            "profile_sidebar_border_color":"87bc44",
            "profile_image_url":"http://a3.twimg.com/profile_images/76229939/
                                 avatar5_normal.jpg",
            "id":5393872,
            "statuses_count":48,
            "utc_offset":3600,
            "created_at":"Sun Apr 22 07:02:54+0000 2007",
            "followers_count":31},
        "id":4887052323,
        "truncated":false,
        "created_at":"Thu Oct 15 12:10:57+0000 2009"}
```

These individual responses will be received by the flow one at a time, as soon as they are available. This is the main idea of streaming APIs: they push events to their clients as they happen. For example, if someone now puts out a tweet containing the keyword *mule*, it will automatically be pushed to our message source instead of being collated and sent as an array when we decide to search for it. Streaming thus provides several benefits: it removes the need to continuously poll the API and worry about rate limiting restrictions, it removes the overhead of the delays between searches to fit in with these restrictions, and it eliminates unnecessary additional processing, such as iterating huge collections and filtering duplicate messages.

WebHooks

Another real-time technology a lot of APIs are using is the a HTTP callback or Web-Hook. The concept is simple: a callback or WebHook is an HTTP POST that occurs when something happens, which makes it a simple event-notification via HTTP POST.

A web application or API implementing this functionality will POST a message to a URL when certain things happen. When a web application enables users to register their own URLs, the users can then extend, customize, and integrate that application with their own custom extensions or even with other applications around the web. For the user, these hooks are a way to receive valuable information when it happens, rather than continually polling for that data and receiving nothing valuable most of the time.

Take an order-based system where you send a request to an API, including a URL that the service provider can send notifications to later as the order changes state, from received to shipped, shipped to delivered, etc. The API can then send you these updates via a WebHook to the URL you specified in the original request.

Although simple, many still currently cringe at the thought of copying URLs, configuring WebHook options, and ensuring security. Cloud Connectors abstract away the fuss of building listeners and of generating and sending URLs around. They provide a consistent and simple interface for configuring all things WebHooks.

Configuring WebHooks

Twilio is a popular infrastructure API that has an excellent WebHook implementation. Twilio uses WebHooks to tell consumers about the status of their requests. When you use Twilio to place a phone call or send an SMS, the Twilio API allows you to send a URL where you'll receive information about the phone call once it ends or the status of the outbound SMS message after it has been processed.

To demonstrate this, we will use the Twilio connector to send an SMS message and then receive updates on its status later via a WebHook. Example 6-9 sends a simple SMS.

Example 6-9. Twilio send SMS

```xml
<?xml version="1.0" encoding="UTF-8"?>
<mule xmlns="http://www.mulesoft.org/schema/mule/core"
    xmlns:twilio="http://www.mulesoft.org/schema/mule/twilio"
    xmlns:spring="http://www.springframework.org/schema/beans"
    xmlns:xsi="http://www.w3.org/2001/XMLSchema-instance"
    xmlns:http="http://www.mulesoft.org/schema/mule/http"
    xsi:schemaLocation="
        http://www.mulesoft.org/schema/mule/twilio
        http://www.mulesoft.org/schema/mule/twilio/current/mule-twilio.xsd
        http://www.springframework.org/schema/beans
        http://www.springframework.org/schema/beans/spring-beans-3.0.xsd
        http://www.mulesoft.org/schema/mule/core
        http://www.mulesoft.org/schema/mule/core/current/mule.xsd
        http://www.mulesoft.org/schema/mule/http
        http://www.mulesoft.org/schema/mule/http/current/mule-http.xsd">

    <twilio:config accountSid="${accountSID}" authToken="${authToken}" />

    <flow name="sendSmsMessage">
        <http:inbound-endpoint address="http://localhost:8080/sendSms" />

        <twilio:send-sms-message
            from="0000000000000" to="0000000000000"
            body="SMS From Mule"  />
    </flow>

</mule>
```

In this example, we first define the connector's `config` element as usual and set the connector's specific attributes: in this case, `accountSid` and `authToken`. These values can be retrieved from the service provider when your register your application.

Next we define our `send-sms-message` operation to send the SMS message via Twilio. The operation accepts three mandatory attributes: `from`, `to`, and `body`. The `from` attribute represents the phone number from which you want to send an SMS. This needs to be an SMS-enabled Twilio phone number, which can be set up through your Twilio account. The `to` attribute represents the phone number to which you want to send an SMS. The `body` attribute contains the body of the message you actually want to send.

This configuration will now send an SMS through the Twilio API. To enable WebHooks, we need a way to create a listener for the callbacks and send Twilio the URL for the listener. To accomplish this, all connector operations that support callbacks will have an optional attribute ending in `-flow-ref` —in this case, `status-callback-flow-ref`. As the name suggests, this attribute should reference a flow. This value must be a valid flow ID from your configuration. It is this flow that will be used to listen for the callback:

```xml
<?xml version="1.0" encoding="UTF-8"?>
<mule xmlns="http://www.mulesoft.org/schema/mule/core"
    xmlns:twilio="http://www.mulesoft.org/schema/mule/twilio"
    xmlns:spring="http://www.springframework.org/schema/beans"
    xmlns:xsi="http://www.w3.org/2001/XMLSchema-instance"
    xmlns:http="http://www.mulesoft.org/schema/mule/http"
    xsi:schemaLocation="
        http://www.mulesoft.org/schema/mule/twilio
        http://www.mulesoft.org/schema/mule/twilio/current/mule-twilio.xsd
        http://www.springframework.org/schema/beans
        http://www.springframework.org/schema/beans/spring-beans-3.0.xsd
        http://www.mulesoft.org/schema/mule/core
        http://www.mulesoft.org/schema/mule/core/current/mule.xsd
        http://www.mulesoft.org/schema/mule/http
        http://www.mulesoft.org/schema/mule/http/current/mule-http.xsd">

    <twilio:config accountSid="${accountSID}" authToken="${authToken}" />

    <flow name="sendSmsMessage">
        <http:inbound-endpoint address="http://localhost:8080/sendSms" />

        <twilio:send-sms-message
            from="0000000000000" to="0000000000000"
            body="SMS From Mule" status-callback-flow-ref="callbackFlow" />
    </flow>

    <flow name="callbackFlow">
        <logger message="Callback received: #[payload]" />
    </flow>

</mule>
```

We have now added the optional `status-callback-flow-ref` attribute and set the value to a matching flow ID: `callbackFlow`. That's nothing out of the ordinary, is it? But wait; notice that the flow `callbackFlow` has no inbound endpoint. Instead, the callback Flow is referenced by the `status-callback-flow-ref` attribute in the send-sms-message processor. This is where the magic happens; when Twilio processes the SMS message, it will automatically send a message to that flow without you having to define an inbound endpoint. The connector automatically generates an inbound endpoint and sends the generated URL to Twilio for you.

Testing WebHooks Locally

For a service provider to call back your application, the application must be accessible to the public Internet. You may find it quicker and easier to work on your local development machine, but these are usually behind firewalls or NAT, or are otherwise not able to provide a public URL. You need a way to make your local web server available to the Internet.

There are a few good services and tools out there to help with this. Examples include ProxyLocal (*http://proxylocal.com/*), and Forward (*https://forwardhq.com/*). Alternatively, you can set up your own reverse SSH Tunnel if you already have a remote system to forward your requests. I find LocalTunnel (*http://progrium.com/localtunnel/*) to be an excellent fit for that need.

LocalTunnel is a simple Ruby Gem that allows you to create a secure route through to your Internet-connected machine, providing a public URL that your development machine behind the firewall can use. With this URL, you can then customize your HTTP callback to work locally. Details on how you customize your HTTP callback URL can be found in "Customizing the Callback" on page 103.

Parsing the Callback

The callback is intended to update us on the status of the SMS message. Within the callback, Twilio will post the following FORM data to your callback URL once the SMS text message has been sent:

```
ACCOUNTSID ********************************
FROM 9177912120
SMSSID SM8b4445c73dbfab696769d5217ac706a6
SMSSTATUS sent
TO 9175557281
```

The request contains the SmsSid, so you can correlate it with the original message, as well as SmsStatus=sent or SmsStatus=failed. But if you run any of the flows we've shown, the callback printed to the console will just be an object reference of a Relea singInputStream. To access the detail of the request we can use the custom HttpRe questBodyToParamMap transformer on our inbound endpoint to return the message properties as a hash map of name-value pairs. This transformer handles GET and POST data with the application/x-www-form-urlencoded content type:

```
<?xml version="1.0" encoding="UTF-8"?>
<mule xmlns="http://www.mulesoft.org/schema/mule/core"
    xmlns:twilio="http://www.mulesoft.org/schema/mule/twilio"
    xmlns:spring="http://www.springframework.org/schema/beans"
    xmlns:xsi="http://www.w3.org/2001/XMLSchema-instance"
    xmlns:http="http://www.mulesoft.org/schema/mule/http"
    xsi:schemaLocation="
```

```
            http://www.mulesoft.org/schema/mule/twilio
            http://www.mulesoft.org/schema/mule/twilio/current/mule-twilio.xsd
            http://www.springframework.org/schema/beans
            http://www.springframework.org/schema/beans/spring-beans-3.0.xsd
            http://www.mulesoft.org/schema/mule/core
            http://www.mulesoft.org/schema/mule/core/current/mule.xsd
            http://www.mulesoft.org/schema/mule/http
            http://www.mulesoft.org/schema/mule/http/current/mule-http.xsd">

    <twilio:config accountSid="${accountSID}" authToken="${authToken}" />

    <flow name="sendSmsMessage">
        <http:inbound-endpoint address="http://localhost:8080/sendSms" />

        <twilio:send-sms-message
            from="0000000000000" to="0000000000000"
            body="SMS From Mule" status-callback-flow-ref="callbackFlow" />
    </flow>

    <flow name="callbackFlow">
        <logger message="Callback received: #[payload]" />

        <http:body-to-parameter-map-transformer />
        <logger message="SMS STATUS: #[payload['SmsStatus']]" level="INFO" />
    </flow>

</mule>
```

Now that the message payload is a map, we can use the `#[payload['SmsStatus']]` expression to extract the values. This expression expects a `java.util.Map` payload object and retrieves a value from the map by passing in the key—in this case, `SmsStatus`.

Customizing the Callback

Customizing the callback URL

The auto-generated URL for the callback URL is built using `localhost` as the host, the `http.port` environment variable or `localPort` value as the port, and a randomly generated UUID string as the path of the URL. If these settings are not suitable, they can be overridden within your connector configuration.

Each connector that accepts HTTP callbacks will provide you with an optional `http-callback-config` child element to override these settings. These settings can be set at the connectors `config` level, as shown in Example 6-10.

Example 6-10. Overriding callback settings

```
<?xml version="1.0" encoding="UTF-8"?>
<mule xmlns="http://www.mulesoft.org/schema/mule/core"
    xmlns:twilio="http://www.mulesoft.org/schema/mule/twilio"
    xmlns:spring="http://www.springframework.org/schema/beans"
```

```
    xmlns:xsi="http://www.w3.org/2001/XMLSchema-instance"
    xmlns:http="http://www.mulesoft.org/schema/mule/http"
    xsi:schemaLocation="
        http://www.mulesoft.org/schema/mule/twilio
        http://www.mulesoft.org/schema/mule/twilio/current/mule-twilio.xsd
        http://www.springframework.org/schema/beans
        http://www.springframework.org/schema/beans/spring-beans-3.0.xsd
        http://www.mulesoft.org/schema/mule/core
        http://www.mulesoft.org/schema/mule/core/current/mule.xsd
        http://www.mulesoft.org/schema/mule/http
        http://www.mulesoft.org/schema/mule/http/current/mule-http.xsd">

    <http:connector name="http" />

    <twilio:config accountSid="${accountSID}" authToken="${authToken}">
        <twilio:http-callback-config
            domain="localhost" localPort="8081"
            remotePort="8081" path="callback" connector-ref="http"  />
      </twilio:config >

    <flow name="sendSmsMessage">
        <http:inbound-endpoint address="http://localhost:8080/sendSms" />

        <twilio:send-sms-message
            from="0000000000000" to="0000000000000"
            body="SMS From Mule" status-callback-flow-ref="callbackFlow" />
    </flow>

    <flow name="callbackFlow">
        <logger message="Callback received: #[payload]" />

        <http:body-to-parameter-map-transformer />

        <logger message="SMS STATUS: #[payload['SmsStatus']]" level="INFO" />
    </flow>

</mule>
```

Example 6-10 amends the previous example to add the additional `http-callback-config` configuration. The configuration takes three mandatory arguments: `domain`, `localPort`, and `remotePort`. These settings will be used to construct the URL that is passed to the external system. The URL will be the same as the default generated URL of the HTTP inbound endpoint, except that the host is replaced by the `domain` setting (or its default value) and the port is replaced by the `remotePort` setting (or its default value).

Securing the callback

Keep in mind that this callback URL is going to be wide open on the Internet, so steps should be taken to secure it. In any case, by default, some service providers will accept only HTTPS endpoints for security purposes.

By default, Mule creates only an HTTP endpoint. This can be overridden by passing in a reference to a predefined HTTPS connector through the optional attribute `connector-ref`.

Example 6-11 amends the previous WebHook example to use the HTTPS protocol for secure callbacks. In this example, we have first defined an additional HTTPS connector via the `https:connector` element. This connector provides secure HTTP connectivity on top of what is already provided with the Mule HTTP transport. More information on using the HTTPS connector and setting up trust stores can be found at the Mule website (*http://bit.ly/1nfBmtK*).

Example 6-11. Secure HTTPS WebHook implementation

```
<?xml version="1.0" encoding="UTF-8"?>
<mule xmlns="http://www.mulesoft.org/schema/mule/core"
    xmlns:twilio="http://www.mulesoft.org/schema/mule/twilio"
    xmlns:spring="http://www.springframework.org/schema/beans"
    xmlns:xsi="http://www.w3.org/2001/XMLSchema-instance"
    xmlns:http="http://www.mulesoft.org/schema/mule/http"
    xmlns:https="http://www.mulesoft.org/schema/mule/https"
    xsi:schemaLocation="
        http://www.mulesoft.org/schema/mule/twilio
        http://www.mulesoft.org/schema/mule/twilio/current/mule-twilio.xsd
        http://www.springframework.org/schema/beans
        http://www.springframework.org/schema/beans/spring-beans-3.0.xsd
        http://www.mulesoft.org/schema/mule/core
        http://www.mulesoft.org/schema/mule/core/current/mule.xsd
        http://www.mulesoft.org/schema/mule/http
        http://www.mulesoft.org/schema/mule/http/current/mule-http.xsd
        http://www.mulesoft.org/schema/mule/https
        http://www.mulesoft.org/schema/mule/https/current/mule-https.xsd">

    <twilio:config accountSid="${accountSID}" authToken="${authToken}">
    <twilio:http-callback-config
        domain="localhost" localPort="8443"
        remotePort="8443" connector-ref="httpsConnector" />
    </twilio:config >

    <https:connector name="httpsConnector">
        <https:tls-key-store path="keystore.jks"
            keyPassword="mule2012" storePassword="mule2012" />
    </https:connector>

    <flow name="sendSmsMessage">
        <http:inbound-endpoint address="http://localhost:8080/sendSms" />
```

```
            <twilio:send-sms-message
                from="0000000000000" to="0000000000000"
                body="SMS From Mule" status-callback-flow-ref="callbackFlow" />
        </flow>

        <flow name="callbackFlow">
            <logger message="Callback received: #[payload]" />

            <http:body-to-parameter-map-transformer />

            <logger message="SMS STATUS: #[payload['SmsStatus']]" level="INFO" />
        </flow>

    </mule>
```

Secondly, we have given the HTTPS connector a unique name via the name attribute to identify the connector. Lastly, the http-callback-config is done exactly as before, with the difference that we have now attached the additional connector-ref attribute to signal which HTTPS connector to use.

Summary

It's about time the Web became more event-driven, and fortunately many service providers are now providing more real-time push-based protocols and technologies for accessing their APIs. However, the inconsistencies and complexities in implementing these APIs can be a real challenge. Throughout this chapter, we have seen how Cloud Connectors help simplify working with these protocols and let you concentrate on working with that lovely real-time data.

CHAPTER 7

Custom Connectivity

Mule Cloud Connect supports a growing number of Cloud Connectors, but new APIs are being released every day and you or your customers might require connectivity to an API that is not currently supported. To help with this, Mule has created a development kit called the DevKit that guides you though the setup and creation of Cloud Connectors. The DevKit uses annotations that mimic typical integration tasks to simplify development and when processed, are converted into fully featured components for the Mule ESB and CloudHub integration platforms. It allows you to quickly and efficiently create new connectors to different cloud services while minimizing the amount of code you have to write.

Cloud Connectors are also about community. Almost all Cloud Connectors are released into the Mule community, and if you've developed a Cloud Connector or want to create one that doesn't exist yet, you can choose to share it with other Mule users like you and help empower the Mule community. If you're a service provider, you can easily convert your existing client libraries to a Cloud Connector and help make a developer's day by getting him up and running with your API fast and painlessly.

Creating Your First Cloud Connector

The Mule DevKit provides excellent tooling to simplify the creation of Mule extensions. It can generate the project with all the necessary dependencies to create a custom Cloud Connector and generate the required directory structure and class skeletons to help you start coding quickly.

Setting Up Your Development Environment

In order to get started building a Cloud Connector, you need to first check that you have a few items. The development kit uses Java and Apache Maven to compile and package your Cloud Connector. It will also install any additional libraries that your connector will require. You do not need to be an experienced user of Maven to use the development kit, as most of the commands are wrapped in simple scripts, but a Java development kit and Maven must be present on your system.

The best way to check to see whether you have Maven installed and set up correctly is to run the following command from your console:

```
mvn -version
```

If you have version 3.x or later of Maven installed, you are all set. Otherwise, please download and install the latest version of Maven.

More information and download links for Maven can be found at the Apache Maven site (*http://maven.apache.org/*).

As mentioned, Java is also required and you should make sure you have a recent software development kit installed (Java 1.6 or later).

Once the JDK and Maven are successfully installed, you will need access to the archetype provided by Mule. The archetype is hosted at Mule's public repositories. To execute it, you will need to add the repository to your Maven's *settings.xml* file:

```
<mirrors>
    <mirror>
      <id>mulesoft-release</id>
      <mirrorOf>mulesoft-release</mirrorOf>
      <name>MuleSoft Release Repository</name>
      <url>http://repository.mulesoft.org/release/</url>
    </mirror>
    <mirror>
      <id>mulesoft-snapshot</id>
      <mirrorOf>mulesoft-snapshot</mirrorOf>
      <name>MuleSoft Snapshot Repository</name>
      <url>http://repository.mulesoft.org/snapshot/</url>
    </mirror>
</mirrors>
```

Generating the Skeleton

With the development environment set up, the DevKit can be used for generating the skeleton project setup with the required classes and libraries you will need. Generating the project is as simple as running a Maven archetype. The archetype script is as follows:

```
mvn archetype:generate -DarchetypeGroupId=org.mule.tools.devkit \
  -DarchetypeArtifactId=mule-devkit-archetype-cloud-connector \
  -DarchetypeVersion=3.3.0 -DgroupId=org.hello -DartifactId=hello-connector
    -Dversion=1.0-SNAPSHOT \
```

```
-DmuleVersion=3.3.0 -DmuleConnectorName=Hello -Dpackage=org.hello \
-DarchetypeRepository=http://repository.mulesoft.org/releases
```

Before running this script, let's first take a look at the various parameters:

muleConnectorName
    The name of your connector

package
    The package under which the skeleton cloud connector will live

artifactId
    The Maven `artifactId` of the connector

groupId
    The Maven `groupId` of the connector

To demonstrate the creation of a cloud connector, we will use the Google Maps API. Example 7-1 amends the parameters in the script to reflect this.

Example 7-1. Create Cloud Connector archetype

```
mvn archetype:generate -DarchetypeGroupId=org.mule.tools.devkit \
 -DarchetypeArtifactId=mule-devkit-archetype-cloud-connector \
 -DarchetypeVersion=3.3.0 -DgroupId=org.mule.module.googlemaps
    -DartifactId=googlemaps-connector -Dversion=1.0-SNAPSHOT \
 -DmuleVersion=3.3.0 -DmuleConnectorName=GoogleMaps
    -Dpackage=org.mule.module.googlemaps \
 -DarchetypeRepository=http://repository.mulesoft.org/releases
```

Once you run this command, you'll be prompted to ensure that the parameters we discussed are correct. Type Y followed by the Enter key to confirm. Afterward you will see that Maven has generated a project for your connector in the target directory containing the following artifacts:

```
googlemaps-connector\LICENSE.md
googlemaps-connector\pom.xml
googlemaps-connector\README.md
googlemaps-connector\doc\GoogleMaps-connector.xml.sample
googlemaps-connector\icons\GoogleMaps-connector-24x16.png
googlemaps-connector\icons\GoogleMaps-connector-48x32.png
googlemaps-connector\icons\GoogleMaps-endpoint-24x16.png
googlemaps-connector\icons\GoogleMaps-endpoint-48x32.png
googlemaps-connector\icons\GoogleMaps-transformer-24x16.png
googlemaps-connector\icons\GoogleMaps-transformer-48x32.png
googlemaps-connector\src\main\app\org\mule\module\googlemaps\plugin.properties
```

```
googlemaps-connector\src\main\java\org\mule\module\googlemaps\
    GoogleMapsConnector.java
googlemaps-connector\src\test\java\org\mule\module\googlemaps\
    GoogleMapsConnectorTest.java
googlemaps-connector\src\test\resources\mule-config.xml
```

The most important of these artifacts is *googlemaps-connector\src\main\java\org\mule \module\googlemaps\GoogleMapsConnector.java.* This is the main connector class where the majority of your code will go. Example 7-2 shows the template or skeleton code generated by Maven.

Example 7-2. Autogenerated class skeleton

```java
/**
 * This file was automatically generated by the Mule Development Kit
 */
package org.mule.module.googlemaps;

import org.mule.api.annotations.Connector;
import org.mule.api.annotations.Connect;
import org.mule.api.annotations.ValidateConnection;
import org.mule.api.annotations.ConnectionIdentifier;
import org.mule.api.annotations.Disconnect;
import org.mule.api.annotations.param.ConnectionKey;
import org.mule.api.ConnectionException;
import org.mule.api.annotations.Configurable;
import org.mule.api.annotations.Processor;

/**
 * Cloud Connector
 *
 * @author MuleSoft, Inc.
 */
@Connector(name="googlemaps", schemaVersion="1.0-SNAPSHOT")
public class GoogleMapsConnector
{
    /**
     * Configurable
     */
    @Configurable
    private String myProperty;

    /**
     * Set property
     *
     * @param myProperty My property
     */
    public void setMyProperty(String myProperty)
    {
        this.myProperty = myProperty;
    }
```

```java
/**
 * Connect
 *
 * @param username A username
 * @param password A password
 * @throws ConnectionException
 */
@Connect
public void connect(@ConnectionKey String username, String password)
    throws ConnectionException {
    /*
     * CODE FOR ESTABLISHING A CONNECTION GOES IN HERE
     */
}

/**
 * Disconnect
 */
@Disconnect
public void disconnect() {
    /*
     * CODE FOR CLOSING A CONNECTION GOES IN HERE
     */
}

/**
 * Are we connected
 */
@ValidateConnection
public boolean isConnected() {
    return true;
}

/**
 * Are we connected
 */
@ConnectionIdentifier
public String connectionId() {
    return "001";
}

/**
 * Custom processor
 *
 * {@sample.xml ../../../doc/GoogleMaps-connector.xml.sample googlemaps:
 *   my-processor}
 *
 * @param content Content to be processed
 * @return Some string
 */
@Processor
```

```
    public String myProcessor(String content)
    {
        /*
         * MESSAGE PROCESSOR CODE GOES HERE
         */

        return content;
    }
}
```

When you inspect the class in Example 7-2, notice that it has autogenerated some basic method stubs and marked them with some specific annotations. These annotations are the key to building your connector. In the next section we will walk though these annotations in detail and introduce some extra annotations to simplify development even further.

Connector Annotations

This section describes what a connector looks like and how you can use annotations to describe your connection.

Connectors

A single annotation appears in the skeleton to determine how the Mule configuration will be generated.

@Connector

Within the generated connector class, the first thing to explain is the @Connector annotation. The DevKit provides this special class-level annotation to tell the annotation processor to export the POJO as a Mule Cloud Connector:

```
@Connector(name="googlemaps", schemaVersion="1.0-SNAPSHOT")
public class GoogleMapsConnector
```

This annotation indicates that a Java class needs to be processed by the DevKit annotation processing tool and considered as a Mule module. The process generates all the required Spring schemas and namespaces so it can be referenced from the Mule configuration.

 Take note of the JavaDoc comments and tags within the connector class. If you make any changes, they will need to be properly documented in order for the DevKit to compile the connector. More information on this can be found in "Documenting Your Connector" on page 122.

This snippet demonstrates the referencing of the generated namespace and schema for the connector. You don't have to create or host this; behind the scenes, the DevKit generated the schema for you and it will be packaged along with the connector:

```xml
<?xml version="1.0" encoding="UTF-8"?>
<mule xmlns="http://www.mulesoft.org/schema/mule/core"
    xmlns:xsi="http://www.w3.org/2001/XMLSchema-instance"
    xmlns:googlemaps="http://www.mulesoft.org/schema/mule/googlemaps"
    xsi:schemaLocation="
        http://www.mulesoft.org/schema/mule/core
        http://www.mulesoft.org/schema/mule/core/current/mule.xsd
        http://www.mulesoft.org/schema/mule/googlemaps
        http://www.mulesoft.org/schema/mule/googlemaps/1.0/mule-googlemaps.xsd">
</mule>
```

Connector Configuration

To designate and control the connector you use, several annotations appear in the skeleton.

@Configurable

As we have seen throughout this book, each connector has a global `config` element where you can set global properties such as credentials, allowing you to pass configurable information to the connector between invocations. Within the connector skeleton, there is already an autogenerated field annotated with the `@Configurable` annotation:

```
@Configurable
private String myProperty;
```

Fields annotated with `@Configurable` can be assigned from Mule. You can annotate as many fields as you want and they can be of any type. These properties can then be assigned from Mule using the `config` element like so:

```xml
<googlemaps:config myProperty="some value" />
```

This allows you to pass in values at the connector level instead of at the operation level, for things like usernames and passwords or other configuration information that does not differ between operation calls.

@Optional

Besides marking fields as `@Configurable`, you can also mark them as `@Optional` if the value is not always required. For example:

```
@Configurable
@Optional
private String myProperty;
```

This declares the argument as optional and allows you to configure the connector with or without the parameter.

@Default

To aid the @Optional annotation, the @Default annotation allows a simple way of providing a default value if an optional parameter is not received. For example:

```
@Configurable
@Optional
@Default("KM")
private String myProperty;
```

The @Default annotation is to be used in conjunction with @Optional and will set the parameter to the default value if no value is passed in from the Mule configuration.

Connector Operations

The annotations in this section control how connections are made.

@Processor

With the default connector in place, we need a way to invoke various API methods. This is done via connector operations or message processors. For each operation you want to perform, the method in your connector class needs to be annotated with @Process or. Methods annotated with @Processor can be invoked from Mule. You can annotate as many methods as you want. These methods can have any type and number of parameters and there is no restriction for the return type. The following example adds a message processor to work with the Google Maps Distance Matrix API. This API provides travel distance and time for a matrix of origins and destinations:

```
/**
 * Custom processor
 *
 * {@sample.xml ../../../doc/GoogleMaps-connector.xml.sample googlemaps:
     my-processor}
 *
 * @param origin The origin from where to calculate the distance from
 * @param destination The destination from where to calculate the distance from
 *
 * @return Some string
 */
@Processor
public String getDistance(String origin, String destination)
```

In this example, we have annotated a simple method signature with the @Processor annotation. We gave it an appropriate name to correspond with the API operation and two arguments for the API parameters: origin and destination. This method can now be invoked from the Mule configuration as follows:

```
<?xml version="1.0" encoding="UTF-8"?>
<mule xmlns="http://www.mulesoft.org/schema/mule/core"
    xmlns:xsi="http://www.w3.org/2001/XMLSchema-instance"
    xmlns:googlemaps="http://www.mulesoft.org/schema/mule/googlemaps"
```

```
xsi:schemaLocation="
    http://www.mulesoft.org/schema/mule/core
    http://www.mulesoft.org/schema/mule/core/current/mule.xsd
    http://www.mulesoft.org/schema/mule/googlemaps
    http://www.mulesoft.org/schema/mule/googlemaps/1.0/mule-googlemaps.xsd">

<googlemaps:config />

<flow name="testFlow">
    <googlemaps:get-distance origin="San+Francisco" destination="Milbrae"/>
</flow>
</mule>
```

The `googlemaps:get-distance` element will now invoke the `getDistance(String origin, String destination)` method. In the configuration, all letters must be lowercase and separated by hyphens. The DevKit will automatically convert method names for you. If your method signature is camel-case, the kit uses each capital letter as the start of a new word and separates words with hyphens.

@Source

Another way to invoke connector operations is via message sources. One particular use of a message source is to implement streaming APIs, whereby the operation is the source of the message rather than a typical request-response style API. A message source is represented by the `@Source` annotation and marks a method inside an `@Connector` annotated class as callable from a Mule flow and capable of generating Mule events. Each marked method has a message source generated for it. The method must receive a `SourceCallback` as one of its arguments that represents the next message processor in the chain. It doesn't matter what order this parameter appears in, as long it is present in the method signature.

Example 7-3 shows a snippet from the Salesforce connector that uses the Salesforce streaming API in which users can subscribe to topics and receive notifications when a new event related to that topic happens.

Example 7-3. @Source annotation example

```
@Source
public void subscribeTopic(String topic, final SourceCallback callback) {
    getBayeuxClient().subscribe(topic, new ClientSessionChannel.MessageListener() {
        @Override
        public void onMessage(ClientSessionChannel channel, Message message) {
            try {
                callback.process(message.getData());
            } catch (Exception e) {
                LOGGER.error(e);
            }
        }
    });
}
```

Connection Management

As discussed in Chapter 5, the DevKit can generate automatic connection management around a connector for connecting, disconnecting, validating connections, and getting a session identifier. These features are provided by the following set of key annotations that mark specific methods within a connector responsible for each of these individual tasks. When generating the connector, the DevKit automatically creates and annotates some default method stubs for you, ready to implement with your own functionality.

@Connect

The @Connect annotation marks a method inside an @Connector as responsible for creating a connection. It will be called by the connector's connection manager every time a connector operation is invoked and is responsible for retrieving existing connections and creating new instances of the connector. There must be exactly one method annotated with @Connect, otherwise compilation will fail:

```
/**
 * Connect
 *
 * @param username A username
 * @param password A password
 * @throws ConnectionException
 */
@Connect
public void connect(@ConnectionKey String username, String password)
    throws ConnectionException {
    /*
     * CODE FOR ESTABLISHING A CONNECTION GOES IN HERE
     */
}
```

Any method annotated with the @Connect annotation must adhere to the following rules:

1. The method signature must be marked `public`.

2. It must throw an `org.mule.api.ConnectionException` and no other exception.

3. Its return type must be `void`.

One important thing to notice is that one of the arguments is annotated with @Connectionkey. It will be used as the key for borrowing and returning objects in the pool. Currently, at least one field must be an @ConnectionKey.

@Disconnect

The @Disconnect annotation marks the method within an @Connector that is responsible for disposing of a connection. It will be called by the connector's connection manager when the connection is no longer needed. If a pooled connector has been sitting idle for too long, it will get automatically evicted from the pool. This annotated method is where you can clean up any connection resources and log out of the service:

```
/**
 * Disconnect
 */
@Disconnect
public void disconnect() {
    /*
     * CODE FOR CLOSING A CONNECTION GOES IN HERE
     */
}
```

There must be exactly one method annotated with @Disconnect, otherwise compilation will fail. Any method annotated with the @Disonnect annotation must adhere to the following rules:

1. The method signature must be marked `public`.

2. It cannot receive any parameters.

3. Its return type must be `void`.

@ValidateConnection

The @ValidateConnection annotation marks the method within an @Connector that is responsible to verify whether the connector is actually connected or not. The connection manager, after retrieving a connector from the pool, will run this method to determine whether the connector is actually valid:

```
/**
 * Are we connected
 */
@ValidateConnection
public boolean isConnected() {
    return true;
}
```

This default method stub always returns the constant value `true`, indicating that the connection is always valid. However, your implementation should use service-specific features to determine whether the connection is actually valid. For example, the following Salesforce connector snippet uses the Salesforce client libraries to determine whether the client is set with a session key:

```
@ValidateConnection
public boolean isConnected() {
    if (bulkConnection != null) {
        if (connection != null) {
            if (loginResult != null) {
                if (loginResult.getSessionId() != null) {
```

```
                    return true;
                }
            }
        }
    }

    return false;
}
```

There must be exactly one method annotated with @ValidateConnection, otherwise compilation will fail. Any method annotated with the @ValidateConnection annotation must adhere to the following rules:

1. The method signature must be marked public.

2. It cannot receive any parameters.

3. It cannot have a return type different than boolean or java.lang.Boolean.

@ConnectionIdentifier

The @ConnectionIdentifier annotation marks the method within an @Connector that is responsible for identifying a connection. It will be called by the connector's connection manager for debugging purposes:

```
/**
 * Are we connected
 */
@ConnectionIdentifier
public String connectionId() {
    return "001";
}
```

This default method stub always return the constant value 001. As this method is used for debugging purposes, this will not be very helpful if all connections have the same identifier. Your implementation should use service specific features to identify individual connections. For example, the following Salesforce connector snippet uses the session ID to identify its connections:

```
/**
 * Returns the session id for the current connection
 *
 * @return the session id for the current connection
 */
@ConnectionIdentifier
public String getSessionId() {
    if (connection != null) {
        if (loginResult != null) {
            return loginResult.getSessionId();
        }
    }
```

```
    return null;
}
```

There must be exactly one method annotated with @ConnectionIdentifier, otherwise compilation will fail. Any method annotated with the @ConnectionIdentifier annotation must adhere to the following rules:

1. The method signature must be marked public.
2. The method signature must not be marked static.
3. It cannot receive any parameters.
4. It must have a return type of java.lang.String.

@InvalidateConnectionOn

The @InvalidateConnectionOn marks the @Processor annotated method that is responsible for invalidating connections under certain error conditions. Although the connection manager attempts to remove idle connections automatically, there may be other scenarios that will cause a connection to expire or become void. This annotation listens for specific exceptions thrown by connector operations that indicate that a connection is no longer valid and removes such connections from the connector pool:

```
@InvalidateConnectionOn(exception = SoapConnection.SessionTimedOut
                                    Exception.class)
```

This annotation is an optional annotation that receives a single argument, exception, which takes the class or list of classes for the specific exceptions that indicate when a connection is no longer valid. On invalidating the connection, the connection manager will automatically call the @Connect method and attempt to retrieve a new connection before retrying the previously failed operation.

Interacting with API

So far we have our skeleton connector that can be invoked from a Mule configuration, but it currently has no interaction with an API. Whether it's the API you have just built or a public service such as Twitter, you will want to be able to interact with it somehow. The logic to interact with an API is up to you and depends on the specific API. If you're interacting with a well-known API, you may have some client libraries you can simply call within your processor, or if you're using SOAP, you probably will want to use the generated client code from a WSDL specification. However, with the rise of RESTful APIs, and seeing as RESTful services work with basic HTTP requests, it is very easy to work with them in a number of different ways. The DevKit provides a set of annotations that simplify the job even further.

First, let's have a quick look at the anatomy of a Rest API. A RESTful HTTP request is made up of the following parts:

URI

> A REST request begins by specifying the resource to be acted on. This resource is identified by its URI. The URI for each resource should be unique. Note that the URI just tells the web service what to act on—the specifics of what action to take and what format to respond in are handled in other parts of the request.

Method

> Each request sent to a RESTful service uses an HTTP method, which determines the action to be taken on the specified resource. Here are four methods commonly used with RESTful services:

> GET
>> Retrieves resources

> PUT
>> Updates resources

> POST
>> Adds new resources

> DELETE
>> Removes resources

Headers

> Request headers provide the server with processing instructions for the current request. Common headers include:

> Accept
>> Determines the response format

> Cache-Control
>> Determines whether or not the server can respond with cached data

> Content-Type
>> Informs the server of the format of the body message, if any

Body

> The body of a request holds additional information in the format specified by the Content-Type header. In a PUT or POST command, the body contains a copy of a new or modified resource to be added to the web service's content.

For each part of the request, the DevKit provides a set of annotations to build and execute your request. The following sections describe in detail the annotation set that enables you to easily work with each part of a REST request.

@RestCall

The `@RestCall` annotation is to be used in conjunction with `@Processor` to indicate that it should make a RESTful request when the method is invoked:

```
@Connector(name="googlemaps", schemaVersion="1.0")
public abstract class GoogleMapsConnector {
    @Processor
    @RestCall(uri = "http://maps.googleapis.com/maps/api/distancematrix/xml?" +
        "origins=San+Francisco&destinations=Milbrae&units=KM&sensor=false",
        method = org.mule.api.annotations.rest.HttpMethod.GET)
    public abstract String getDistance() throws IOException;
}
```

The annotation has two compulsory arguments for the URI and method attributes of the request: `uri` and `method`. The example just shown uses the full URI and parameters as the URI argument. Setting the URI parameters dynamically will be covered shortly. After setting the URI, we then set the method to use the `GET` HTTP method. Here we are using the value from the `org.mule.api.annotations.rest.HttpMethod` class, which has a set of static fields for all available HTTP methods.

The message processor, when annotated, must have a return type of `java.lang` `.String`, must throw an `IOException`, and must be declared `abstract`. And as Java dictates, if the class contains an abstract method, the class must be also marked abstract.

@RestQueryParam

Query parameters are the most common type of parameter that are appended to the path of the URL when submitting a request. You can see them added to the base URI after a ? or & symbol. These variable parameters—in this case, `origin` and `distance`—are probably never going to be static, so we need a way to map values to these from method arguments. To enable us to pass these in programmatically, method arguments can automatically be bound to URIs using the `@RestQueryParam` annotation. This annotation is used to mark method arguments that will be appended to the URI. The annotation takes a single argument for the String representation of the parameter name to be appended. For example:

```
@Connector(name="googlemaps", schemaVersion="1.0")
public abstract class GoogleMapsConnector {
    @Processor
    @RestCall(uri = "http://maps.googleapis.com/maps/api/distancematrix/xml",
        method = org.mule.api.annotations.rest.HttpMethod.GET)
    public abstract String getDistance(@RestQueryParam("origins")
        String origin, @RestQueryParam("destinations")
        String destination, @RestQueryParam("sensor") Boolean sensor)
            throws Exception;
}
```

This will now append the two query parameters to the base URI and populate their values with the values passed in the method arguments.

@RestUriParam

On top of query parameters, some URIs also require parameters that are actually made part of the path, not parameters appended to the end of the URI. For example, the Google Maps URI provides an /xml variable path value for the format of the response. To enable you to pass these in programmatically, the URI attribute within the @RestCall annotation supports *template parameters*. Template parameters are a flexible way of parameterizing the actual path of the request, which allow you to provide a placeholder to be overwritten by a variable value. This can be set up as follows:

```
@Connector(name="googlemaps", schemaVersion="1.0")
public abstract class GoogleMapsConnector {
    @Processor
    @RestCall(uri = "http://maps.googleapis.com/maps/api/distancematrix/{
                    format}",
        method = org.mule.api.annotations.rest.HttpMethod.GET)
    public abstract String getDistance(@RestUriParam(value = "format")
        String format,
        @RestQueryParam("origins") String origin,
        @RestQueryParam("destinations") String destination,
    @RestQueryParam("sensor") Boolean sensor) throws IOException;
}
```

We have now replaced the value for the format with a variable name surrounded with curly braces. This will indicate that these values need to be bound on invocation.

Now that we have the template in place, we need to tell the message processor to bind certain values to the template parameters in the URI. This is done via the @RestUriParam annotation. For each template parameter you want to bind, you must annotate an argument to the message processor with the @RestUriParam annotation. This will now bind the values passed into the method arguments to the template parameters in the URI.

Documenting Your Connector

In order to compile and generate the connector, the DevKit requires a minimum set of JavaDoc comments and tags for code that utilize certain DevKit annotations. These tags will then produce a simple and elegant tab-based website complete with an installation guide, JavaDocs, and example code.

Connectors

Each class annotated with @Connector must have a class-level JavaDoc comment with a high-level overview of the connector and must include an @author tag detailing the author of the connector:

```
/**
 * Cloud Connector
```

```
 *
 * @author MuleSoft, Inc.
 */
@Connector(name="googlemaps", schemaVersion="1.0-SNAPSHOT")
public class GoogleMapsConnector
```

Configurable Fields

Each field annotated with `@Configurable` is required to have a JavaDoc comment briefly explaining what this attribute is used for:

```
/**
 * Configurable
 */
@Configurable
private String myProperty;
```

Message Processors

Each method annotated with `@Processor` and `@Source` must have a JavaDoc comment detailing each and every parameter using the `@param` tag and must also detail the return type using the `@return` tag, if the method's return type is anything but `void`. It must also declare any exception being thrown using the `@throws` tag and provide a description of the exception being thrown:

```
/**
 * Custom processor
 *
 * {@sample.xml ../../../doc/GoogleMaps-connector.xml.sample googlemaps:
     my-processor}
 *
 * @param content Content to be processed
 * @return Some string
 * @throws Exception exception description
 */
@Processor
public String myProcessor(String content) throws Exception
```

Sample XML

Also notice the `@sample.xml` tag within the JavaDoc body. The DevKit uses this tag to analyze the content of a snippet introduced in the source code:

```
@sample.xml ../../../doc/GoogleMaps-connector.xml.sample googlemaps:my-processor
```

The tag is followed by a filepath relative to the connector and then subsequently followed by a pointer to a particular snippet within that file. Each method annotated with `@Pro cessor` and `@Source` must contain this tag within its JavaDoc body and the value must point to a snippet within a valid sample XML file. The DevKit will automatically generate a sample file and snippet for the default generated message processor. In this case, the file is *../../../doc/GoogleMaps-connector.xml.sample*. Each snippet should show how to invoke a particular message processor or source from within the Mule configuration XML. When you inspect this file, you will see that the sample method `public String myProcessor(String content)` has an associated snippet similar to the following:

```
<!-- BEGIN_INCLUDE(googlemaps:my-processor) -->
    <googlemaps:my-processor content="#[map-payload:content]" />
<!-- END_INCLUDE(googlemaps:my-processor) -->
```

The DevKit will not execute the XML, though it does ensure that the XML sample parses successfully against the generated schema.

Generating the Documentation

Using this JavaDoc, the DevKit generates the documentation by running a simple Maven command:

```
mvn javadoc:javadoc
```

This command generates the documentation and places it in the *target/apidocs* directory. If you navigate to this directory, there will be a file named *index.html*. Opening this file in a browser should display your connector's documentation and code samples in a tab-based website similar to Figure 7-1.

Building Your Connector

As the final step in creating a Mule connector, you have to build and distribute it. That's all covered in this section.

Packaging Your Connector

Once you're ready to build your connector, the DevKit provides a simple Maven command to build and package it. This can be run by navigating to the connector's target directory and running the following command:

```
mvn package -Ddevkit.studio.package.skip=false
```

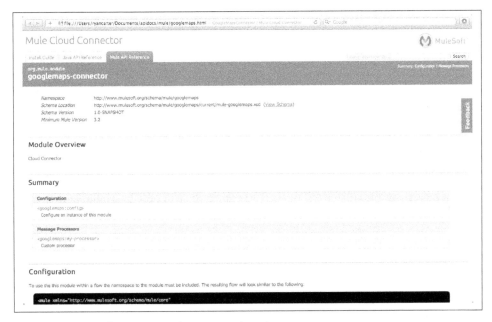

Figure 7-1. Sample connector documentation site

Once run, the DevKit Maven plugin will build several different artifacts for you in the target directory:

googlemaps-connector-1.0-SNAPSHOT.jar
    The connector *JAR* file

googlemaps-connector-1.0-SNAPSHOT.zip
    The connector packaged as a Mule plugin *ZIP* file

apidocs
    Generated installation instructions, JavaDoc, and Mule API docs for your connector

Installing Your Connector

With the generated artifacts in place, installing the connector is pretty much the same as detailed in "Installing Cloud Connectors" on page 15. If you are using Maven, you can add the artifacts to your own repository and add a dependency to you *pom.xml* file. You can also extract the *JAR* file of the connector and its dependencies to your project or Mule installation manually. However, If you are using MuleStudio, you can take advantage of the Update Site feature to also install a connector from your local filesystem. The amended steps are as follows:

1. Click Help → Install New Software on the Mule menu bar.

2. After the Install window opens, click Add, which is located to the right of the "Work with" field.

3. Enter a unique name of your choice for the update site in the Name field (for example, "Google Maps Connector").

4. In the Location field, enter the full path to your connector, prefixed by *file:/*, and click OK.

5. A table will appear displaying the available connectors under "community" and "standard," the newest version, and the connector. Click the available version, then click Next, and finally click Finish. The connector will now be available to import into your project.

After following the onscreen instructions, you will be asked to restart your IDE. After you complete the procedure, the connector will be available to all your Mule applications.

Publishing Your Connector

After you have created a new connector, you can submit it as a project on MuleForge. This allows you to share it with the Mule community so you can get feedback on the quality and design of the connector before putting it into production. By submitting to the MuleSoft site (*http://www.MuleSoft.org*), you get the benefit of others trying out your module, and others get the benefit of your work. Just as you make use of the available connectors in MuleForge that were submitted by others, the connector you have created can be very helpful for them.

In order to make your connector available to the community, fill in the form at the Contribute a Project page (*http://www.mulesoft.org/contribute-project*). Enter as many details as possible, since some of this data will be made public for people searching for Mule connectors and can help them decide whether your connector is the right one for them.

You have to include a link to the source code repository, so make sure the latest code is available at the time you submit the form. The preferred source code repository is GitHub (*https://github.com/*). Also provide a link to the connectors' documentation. The documentation should be as complete as possible to help users start using your connector.

This form will be reviewed and you will receive an email shortly with a confirmation that your connector has been made available in the MuleSoft site.

Going Further

In this chapter we have shown how you can take advantage of the DevKit and start building your own Cloud Connector. But remember, there's a lot more to the DevKit for simplifying integration even further, with specific annotations for OAuth, Web-Hooks, and much more.

And don't forget the community. Almost all Cloud Connectors are released into the Mule community, and if you've developed a Cloud Connector or want to create one that doesn't exist yet, you can choose to share it with other Mule users like you and help empower the Mule community. Need inspiration? Source code for all community Cloud Connectors can be found on GitHub (*https://github.com/mulesoft*). Or need some help? The community is there for you at the MuleSoft forum (*http://forum.mulesoft.org/mule soft*).

About the Author

Ryan Carter is a Solution Architect specializing in integration and APIs. Ryan is passionate about open source and is an appointed Mule champion regularly contributing to the community.

Get even more for your money.

Join the O'Reilly Community, and register the O'Reilly books you own. It's free, and you'll get:

- $4.99 ebook upgrade offer
- 40% upgrade offer on O'Reilly print books
- Membership discounts on books and events
- Free lifetime updates to ebooks and videos
- Multiple ebook formats, DRM FREE
- Participation in the O'Reilly community
- Newsletters
- Account management
- 100% Satisfaction Guarantee

Signing up is easy:

1. Go to: oreilly.com/go/register
2. Create an O'Reilly login.
3. Provide your address.
4. Register your books.

Note: English-language books only

To order books online:
oreilly.com/store

For questions about products or an order:
orders@oreilly.com

To sign up to get topic-specific email announcements and/or news about upcoming books, conferences, special offers, and new technologies:
elists@oreilly.com

For technical questions about book content:
booktech@oreilly.com

To submit new book proposals to our editors:
proposals@oreilly.com

O'Reilly books are available in multiple DRM-free ebook formats. For more information:
oreilly.com/ebooks

Getting Started with Mule Cloud Connect

Connect your enterprise to a wide range of SaaS platforms, Open APIs, and social networks quickly and without difficulty. Through step-by-step instructions and numerous real-world examples, this concise guide shows you how to seamlessly integrate the external services you need with Mule ESB and its powerful Cloud Connect toolset.

You'll learn how to use service-specific connectors for many popular APIs—including Salesforce, Twitter, LinkedIn, and Twilio—through easy-to-learn abstractions. If Mule doesn't have a connector for the resource you need, you'll learn how to build your own. You'll discover how easy it is to reach beyond the enterprise firewall for a host of Internet resources.

- Discover the advantages of using Mule Cloud Connect over typical web service clients and protocols
- Learn how Cloud Connectors eliminate the need to understand the underlying API of each service
- Get started with the latest real-time technologies, including REST, WebHooks, and Streaming APIs
- Integrate OAuth secure APIs and understand their role in authorization and information sharing
- Delve into advanced topics such as multi-tenancy and connection management
- Build your own custom connectors with the Mule DevKit

Purchase the ebook edition of this O'Reilly title at oreilly.com and get free updates for the life of the edition. Our ebooks are optimized for several electronic formats, including PDF, EPUB, Mobi, and DAISY—all DRM-free.

Twitter: @oreillymedia
facebook.com/oreilly

US $17.99   CAN $18.99
ISBN: 978-1-449-33100-9

O'REILLY®
oreilly.com